BLACK TIE OPTIONAL

BLACK TIE OPTIONAL

The Ultimate Guide to
Planning and Producing
Successful Special Events

HARRY A. FREEDMAN
with Karen Feldman Smith

FUND RAISING INSTITUTE
A Division of The Taft Group
Rockville, Maryland

Published by
Fund Raising Institute
A Division of The Taft Group
12300 Twinbrook Parkway, Suite 450
Rockville, Maryland 20852
(301) 816-0210

Printed in the United States of America

96 95 94 93 92   6 5 4 3 2

Library of Congress Catalog Card Number: 91-070500
ISBN 0-930807-17-0

Fund Raising Institute publishes books on fund raising, philanthropy, and
nonprofit management. To request sales information, or a copy of our catalog,
please write us at the above address or call 1-800-877-TAFT.

Contents

List of Figures

Introduction

In any community of even modest size, there are dozens of special events a month. A special event is anything that brings groups of people together—the swearing-in of a mayor, a church concert, a black-tie charity ball, or a beach bash. Some are held to raise money, others to build a constituency. No matter the purpose, all require competent planning to be successful.

Besides getting invited to them, many people wind up serving on a committee or helping to organize an event. In some cases, a committee is already in place and records exist of past events—names of vendors, possible sites, budgets, and maybe even reports of what worked and what didn't.

But sometimes it's a first-time event, one for which there's no precedent. This is often the case when a perennial event loses its luster and you need something new to revitalize fund raising. What type of event should it be? What will it cost? How will you attract people and money to it? How much should you charge? Where should you hold it? This book will answer these questions as well as the most important one: Should you even attempt a special event at all?

A special event is like a business. If it is not run that way, it is bound to lose money. But unlike successful businesses, many special events are run by inexperienced people, often volunteers with good intentions but unrealistic expectations. No matter what type of event it is, there are basic ingredients required to make it a success. Chief among them are adequate manpower, good financial management, and a highly organized game plan.

These are the same elements that have raised money and rallied support for various causes since recorded history began, and perhaps before that. When Christopher Columbus wanted to sail in search of new frontiers, his friends and family refused to help pay for his farfetched plan. But he convinced Spain's Queen Isabella and, in a 15th-century version of corporate underwriting, she agreed to bankroll the expedition.

While that was more of a direct appeal for support, many organizations have long used special events as a means of raising money. For centuries, charitable fund raising was an activity limited to the upper classes, who used socials and symphonies and such to fund their pet causes. With the advent of federal income taxes in the early 1900s, and the subsequent write-offs created for charitable giving, the rich had more incentive than ever to contribute. At the time, their choices were limited. Other than churches and museums, there were few nonprofit organizations to which they could donate.

But since World War II, the number of such organizations has climbed from fewer than 1,000 in the late 1940s, to 200,000 in 1980 and more than 480,000 in 1990. The public gave $114.7 billion to nonprofit groups in 1989, according to the American Association of Fund-Raising Counsel. More than half of that went to religious groups. And of the total donated, the vast majority— $96 billion—came from individuals.

The nature and scope of fund raising has changed over the years, too. The rich used to attend to such matters at lavish affairs for a select few. Today, a fund raiser can be a global event, such as Live Aid, the 1986 concert held simultaneously in London and Philadelphia and broadcast around the world. It raised $72 million to feed the starving people of Africa. (A single record by a group of British rock stars calling themselves Band Aid raised another $11 million for the cause.) Live Aid led to a number of other large-scale fund raising efforts: Farm Aid, Sport Aid, Comic Relief, and Hands Across America, among them.

While the concept of fund raising isn't new, never has the need for money been so great. The amount of federal and state help available to social service groups has not kept pace with the rising demand. Tax law changes in 1986 reduced corporate tax incentives for charitable giving. A leaner economy makes it that much more difficult for businesses to give. More and more, it will be up to individual groups to come up with creative ways to raise money.

When I first began fund raising in 1970, I would have benefited immensely from having a how-to guide to help me, but there was no such thing. In 20 years as a professional fund raiser, I've learned a lot, sometimes by making mistakes. I've also developed some basic strategies to help create successful events. This book is a compilation of those strategies which, when used together, should enable anyone to handle projects with greater skill and confidence.

Besides offering easy-to-understand techniques, this book provides checklists for quick reference and worksheets to help plan budgets, set ticket prices, and organize committees. It gives events planners the resources to gain access to big-name entertainment, book them for events, and still manage to make a profit. It offers suggestions for creative special events and relates a number of stories to illustrate how these work. There is no magic to creating a successful event; it just takes organization, manpower, a realistic budget, lots of patience, and hard work. By reading this book and using the worksheets and checklists, you should be able to determine whether your group has the resources required to carry out a successful event. If you decide to produce one, the step-by-step guide should help you maximize your fund-raising potential.

Chapter 1

Choosing An Event

A special event without a purpose is like a racehorse with bad legs: He may have the will to run, but he isn't going to win. That's why the first order of business is to figure out why you want to stage an event. There are two main reasons to go to the trouble: 1) to raise money or 2) to raise the organization's profile and, in so doing, gain new members for future support.

To organize even a moderately scaled event requires a good idea, plus the manpower and money necessary to execute it. The simplest event requires invitations, a location, and all sorts of incidentals that quickly add up (more on that later).

In selecting an event, first figure out who you want to attract. If you hope to bring in young people, an appearance by the Lawrence Welk Dancers won't fill the hall. Likewise, a rap concert will not interest an older crowd. If you want to attract a variety of ages and economic classes, pick an event with broad appeal. That's most often what you should seek since older people usually are the major contributors, but younger ones are needed to keep the organization vital. If you cannot design one event for everyone, try to hold separate ones aimed at each age group (perhaps a dinner/

5

dance with a big band for older people and a beach party with rock bands for younger people).

How do you choose an event that will be successful? First, find something that will be fun, something likely to excite the people you want to attract. Dinners and dances are by far the most common fund raisers, but there's no reason to limit yourself to conventional events. Only your budget, manpower, and imagination limit what you can do.

In New Haven, Connecticut, for example, the Emmaus Monastic Community, a nonsectarian religious group, organized a baseball team of homeless men to play in the local league. The purpose of the team, called the Soupers, was both to raise money for homeless shelters and soup kitchens and to raise public awareness of the city's homeless population. The first season's games raised $2,000 in donations from spectators and rival teams.

The National Kidney Foundation of Upstate New York raised $25,000 with a touch-a-thon. Contestants gathered around a car and competed to see who could continue to touch it for the longest time; the winner got the car. The touch-a-thon participants were the 30 people who raised the most money for the foundation (the average participant raised $700). A local auto dealer donated the car; runners-up got vacations and other donated prizes. This fund raiser, which lasted more than 72 hours, generated a great deal of publicity for the foundation, not to mention $25,000.

Marketing

In order to be successful, you have to know what the public wants and what you are equipped to offer. That's where market research comes in. Market research is every bit as important to a charity as it is to a for-profit business. You are out to make money, just like any other business, or you will be forced to close down. Apply the same rules of operation to your charity that you do to any other financial undertaking. Long before you decide to sponsor an event, examine your community's tastes and spending habits.

You should also look closely at your organization. How big a volunteer base do you have? How much experience at fund raising?

What events have you already done successfully? Who attended? How much access does your group have to corporate sponsors? Do you need to raise money or is exposure more important for your cause right now? Have you successfully conveyed to the public why your cause is a worthwhile one? Why should people give their money to you?

Besides fund-raising events, you should have in place a regular program of news releases, and radio and television public service announcements. Hold periodic information meetings for the public, sponsor a support group, have group members host small gatherings in their homes to introduce more people to your cause. Do this regularly to keep the organization visible in the community. That way, when you hold fund raisers, you can concentrate on raising money without having to spend a lot of time educating people about your charity.

When you are out to raise money, you have to sell more than your group's image; you are selling a product—tickets. A first-time event should be the sort community members normally would attend if it weren't for charity. That makes promotion easier. It also helps if you have something unusual planned, such as a special guest speaker or themed dinner.

If you were going to launch a new product, you would try it out on a few people to determine whether anyone would be interested in buying it. You should do the same thing with an event. Take a fact sheet—listing the who, what, where, and why of the event you are considering—and pass it around. (Figure 1-1 illustrates such a fact sheet.) Ask people's opinions. Would they attend? If not, what would you need to change in order for them to want to attend? Would they pay $150 apiece to attend? If not, how much would they pay?

One way to ensure attendance is to take advantage of something that's in demand. Joe's Stone Crabs, a popular Miami Beach restaurant, is an example. It's usually filled to capacity and there's always a wait for tables. As a fund raiser for Informed Families (part of the Just Say No To Drugs effort), owners Irwin and Joann Sawitz donate the whole restaurant, staff, and food to the charity for the final night of stone-crab season. People know they won't have to wait for a table that night so it always sells out quickly. An event

Figure 1-1. Sample Fact Sheet

SCHOOL OF MEDICINE

1989 GRAND PRIX GALA

FACT SHEET

WHEN: Friday, March 3, 1989
             7:30 in the evening

WHERE: Omni International Hotel

WHY: To benefit the University of Miami/Jackson Memorial
             Burn Center, The Mailman Center for Child Development
             and The Learning Experience School

HOW: An evening which includes

                    * a spectacular cocktail reception
                      with celebrity entertainment

                    * Dinner and dancing

                    * ROBERTA FLACK IN CONCERT

             An excellent way to kick off the Grand Prix Weekend
             while giving support to three of South Florida's
             premiere charities.

DONATION: Patron (per person) $150   Table of ten $1,500.

             Benefactor (Preferred Seating)
                  (per person) $250   Table of ten $2,500

             Corporate Table   Table of ten $3,500
                  (includes two Grand Prix VIP Club memberships)

Checks made payable to GRAND PRIX GALA

All donations are tax deductible as provided by law

For further information contact:

             Harry A. Freedman or Celia Chin Quee 547-6256
             Carole Christoff 547-6395

                    Office of Development for Medical Affairs
                         P.O. Box 016960 (R100)
                         Miami, Florida 33101
                            (305) 547-6256

such as this would not require market research because it has already proven to be popular.

Sample Events

Following are some ideas for fund raisers (listed alphabetically). Each description includes some of the plusses and minuses of the event, a basic idea of the staff and planning time needed, and the earning potential of each, based on what similar events have raised. How much you raise will depend largely on the size and scale of your event and the dedication and talent of those involved.

Don't immediately dismiss the smaller events, because you consider them unworthy of the effort you'll have to expend. It might be more lucrative and less taxing to you, your staff, and volunteers to do a small event once a month, making $500 to $1,000 each time, rather than spending six months on one huge event that might only make $3,000. This is especially true in tight economic times, when people are less inclined to attend big-ticket balls and concerts. Before deciding on a particular event, try to go to a similar one staged by another organization to see how that group handles it and what it should look like. Talk with that group's event planners to find out what was involved.

Obviously, all the possible events aren't listed here, but these will give you something to start with.

Antique Shows

Gather as many area antique dealers as possible, charge each for a booth. Charge a small admission fee to the public. Sell food and beverages. Manpower: minimal (one person to round up vendors, another to manage the site and publicity). Planning time: two months for a small one, up to a year for a big one. Earning potential: $500–$100,000.

Arts & Crafts Show

These can be small, simple affairs, featuring homemade crafts, to big and grandiose, such as Miami Beach's Art Deco Weekend, which attracts 200,000 people. A small one could be put together in a couple of months, while large events like Art Deco Weekend are year-round projects. Manpower: a small show can be handled by two people—one to sign up artists, one to handle staging; a large show might require a committee of 50, each of whom chairs a smaller committee. Earning potential: $1,000–$50,000.

A-Thons

A-thons can involve aerobics, bowling, car racing, car touching, bicycling, running, rocking, hair cutting, jumping, dancing, kissing, swimming, skating, skateboarding, walking, wheelchairing. Each participant gets people to pledge money based on how long he or she does the prescribed activity or his or her score (10 cents per bowling pin or swimming lap, $5 per mile run, etc.). The more participants (divided into groups, each with a captain), the greater the amount collected. If it's an outside activity, however, weather can ruin it. Remember that many groups use this type of event and it can be overdone. Check to see if a lot of other, better-established groups are planning one. If so, consider changing your event. Manpower: moderate (a lot of phone call follow-up involved, team captains, route controllers). These events work best if tied in with a newspaper or radio promotion and tend to grow over time. Costs: moderate (pledge forms, licensing, permits, prizes, T-shirts). Lead time: three months. Earning potential: $1,000–$200,000.

Auctions

These can involve celebrities, tickets to sporting events, cars, bachelors/bachelorettes, travel, food, restaurants, etc. This is perhaps the most labor-intensive type of fund raiser, especially if there are lots of items and you plan both silent and live auctions. Lots of volunteers are needed to line up items, set up and work the room, and make sure the people with money have a reason to come. *The Auction Book* by Betsy Beatty and Libby Kirkpatrick (Auction Press, 1984) explains in detail how to do this. Lead time: six months or more. Advance money needed for invitations, program book, mailing, postage. You may have to rent a storage place to keep donated items. Earning potential: $1,000–$700,000.

Balloon Races

You need a number of elements simultaneously for this one: a big open field, a number of hot-air balloonists willing to participate, good weather (no wind), a good crowd. Sell sponsorships of balloons and charge admission to watch. Sell food and hold a raffle. This could be risky first-time event, especially if bad weather wipes it out. Manpower: minimal (two people). To make this event a success, a major corporate sponsor is a necessity. Sometimes a new hotel, store, or radio or television station is willing to pay for the event, with proceeds going to the charity. A prime spot for this event is the site of shopping mall before construction starts. Planning time: three months. Earning potential: $500–$10,000.

Beach Party

Hold a giant party with live music on the beach. Generally, the hardest part of this event is getting the permits, since most beaches are government controlled. Line up some big-name bands and vendors to sell refreshments. Get a radio or television station to broadcast live to encourage greater turnout. Charge admission. Not much upfront money is needed, especially if corporate sponsors pay for booths, T-shirts, etc. Planning time: four to five months. The biggest risk is the weather. Manpower: high. You need a lot of people the day of the event to handle security, man booths, sell food and T-shirts, control the crowd, collect tickets, etc. The big money-maker is often the beer concession, so a beer sponsor can make a big difference, especially if the distributor will donate part of the beer to your group. This is an ideal activity for building a young leadership group within your organization. (Even if you don't live anywhere near a beach, you can do this. Haul a load of sand in and make your own beach.) Earning potential: $500–$10,000.

Bingo/Casino Nights

These aren't legal everywhere, so check first. In areas where they are legal, there often are bingo halls—places that do nothing but run bingo games. Every session must be for the benefit of a charity. Perhaps one near you has an evening or day's worth of games open for your group to sponsor. To do this, a volunteer from the charity must be in attendance, making manpower requirements minimal. Staff requirements would be heavier if there are no such halls and you have to produce a game on your own.

Casino nights can be quite lucrative, but to be done right they almost always require a professional company that produces such events. By the time you rent the equipment and hire the dealers, you'd probably spend more money and time than it would cost to hire a firm that routinely handles these and does them well. It's fairly expensive but easy; basically, you are buying an event. All your group must do is get prizes, printing, and publicity and sell tickets. Lead time: four months. Earning potential: $500–$15,000.

Business Opening

Any kind of business, such as a department store, restaurant, supermarket, or office building. Sometimes you can arrange for the company's staff and advertising firm to handle the details of the event. All you have to do is provide the right monied people to attend. In return, many businesses will pay for printing, ads, giveaways, sometimes even food (that's negotiable). The major role of your group will be to contact and encourage the proper people to attend. Money is raised by charging admission or based on a percentage of sales. The more successful you are, the more likely your chance will be to participate in future openings. If you can't produce 600 affluent people for a grand opening, don't attempt this. Obviously, this is an easy and effective event, so many charities want it. You have to have a top-notch proposal and the ability to back it up with people and money (and, even better, a celebrity; see chapter 6) to compete with the other charities that want the same thing. Planning time: three months. Earning potential: $500–$100,000.

Celebrity Appearance

Finding a celebrity (author, athlete, etc.) willing to appear at a price you can afford is the key to success. Make sure you have good legal advice and adequate volunteers to sell tickets. This is not a good choice for the inexperienced. A lot of money is needed up front for advertising and deposits. Manpower: high. Groups new to large-scale fund raising might want to purchase a block of tickets to an appearance someone else is producing, then sell them at a higher price, the difference going toward the charity. Planning time: six months minimum. Boost fund raising by holding a meet-the-author/athlete/etc. reception following the talk for an additional fee. Earning potential: $1,000–$25,000.

Chili Cookoff

Link up with a regional or national chili competition and line up contestants, each of whom pays to compete, and find a place to hold it. If you allow the public to purchase samples, health department guidelines must be met and a permit acquired. Manpower: moderate. There must be a committee to sign up competitors and another (larger) one to handle publicity, site acquisition, entertainment, security, parking, etc. Charge admission and for parking. Hold a raffle, giving away donated prizes. Getting a radio station to sponsor is helpful, as is a corporate sponsor who might pay for entertainment. This is not a job for a two-person office. Planning time: four to six months. Earning potential: $1,000–$30,000.

Concert (local talent)

Like carnivals, these more often boost public awareness of a charity, rather than raise large amounts of money. These can be held in the school auditorium or church sanctuary and publicized in a school or church newsletter. To boost fund raising, a bake or candy sale or raffle can be held at the same time. Planning time: four to six weeks. Earning potential: $100–$1,000.

Concert (celebrity)

Bringing in the stars takes a lot of time, manpower, money, and legal advice. This is not a good choice for the inexperienced. Even an experienced group can fail at this if the public decides not to attend. A lot of money is needed up front for advertising and deposits. Manpower: high. A lot of people are needed to sell tickets (or you have to hire a ticket-selling service or both). Groups just starting out at this might want to purchase a block of tickets to a concert someone else is producing, then sell them at a higher price, the difference going to the charity. Planning time: six months minimum. Earning potential: $1,000–$500,000.

Cooking Demonstration

Arrange appearances of chefs at local department stores (hold in the housewares department) or restaurants, when the establishment is normally closed. People pay a fee ($25 or so) to see the demonstration. The charity might also get a percentage based on the amount of merchandise sold during the show. To boost income, have cookbook authors on hand to autograph books. The charity might get a percentage of book sales, too. Manpower: minimal. Costs are minimal, too (sometimes the department store or restaurant will cover or contribute to printing costs for invitations and/or posters). Earning potential: $250–$1,000.

Costume Party

These can be based on a theme (end of the decade, television characters, card decks, colors) or occasion (Halloween, New Year's Eve, Mardi Gras, Christmas in July). Manpower: minimal to moderate. You need invitations, refreshments, a site, some publicity. Earning potential: $500–$150,000.

Country Fair, Carnival, Street Fair

Have an assortment of booths, featuring arts and crafts, food, music (appearances by school choirs, orchestras, and marching bands help get more people involved). This event is more a friend raiser, than a money-maker, but it's a good way to start building visibility. Planning time: one or two months. If this can be tied in with another organization's festival or "a-thon" (see above), it's likely to raise some money. Sometimes municipalities help sponsor such events, perhaps supplying a park or recreation center at which to hold it. Volunteers can put together the booths. Other events that boost attendance include 4-H displays, pig or crab races. Earning potential: $500–$20,000.

Cow Chip Bingo

Take one football field, divide it into one-square-yard plats and sell them for $20 each (including barbecue dinner). On the specified night, have one well-fed cow wander the field. The winner (of $10,000 if you sell all the plats) is the holder of plat in which the cow drops its chips. Charge admission to the event (for non-plat holders), sell refreshments and give away prizes. Advance expenses are minimal. Manpower: moderate. Planning time: eight weeks. Earning potential: $5,000–$50,000.

Cruise

Plan A—A full cruise. Hook up with a cruise line or travel agent to sell tickets on a particular cruise. A percentage of each cruise sold goes to the charity. Aim for a longer, more exotic cruise for older people with more disposable income, a shorter, less expensive cruise for younger people. Manpower: minimal. Planning time: four to six months. Earning potential: $1,500–$50,000.

Plan B—Charter a boat for a day. Rent out the whole ship for a day-long cruise to nowhere (cruise lines are most happy to do this when launching a new ship or relaunching a refurbished one). Planning time: four to six months. Manpower: minimal. Earning potential: $5,000–$50,000.

Plan C—A meal on board. Sometimes cruise lines will donate a meal to a charity to get potential customers on board. Your group brings in the people, the cruise line does the rest. Remember that this event is limited to the number of seats in the ship's dining room. Manpower: minimal. Planning time: two months. Earning potential: $500–$5,000.

Dance

A dance could revolve around any theme—'50s–'60s, big band, country/western, square, polka, rock, rap. Without a meal involved, these are relatively easy to do. You need a place to hold it, music (live or recorded), light refreshments, and announcements. Sometimes a local radio station will serve as sponsor. This is not usually a big money-maker, but profits can be increased with a raffle (if legal). Manpower: minimal. Planning time: four to eight weeks. Earning potential: $200–$5,000.

Dine-Arounds

Arrange to have each of three to six restaurants prepare one course for a progressive meal. Diners pay a fee and travel from place to place for each course. A variation is to have several restaurants each offer a meal and cooking demonstration on a different night. Diners may buy seats at one or all the restaurants. Sometimes restaurants donate a course or portion of a meal, allowing the charity to keep more of the money raised. Raise more by holding a raffle or auction at the same time. Another form of dine-around takes place in one spot but diners change tables for each course. This is a good singles event. Manpower: minimal. Earning potential: $500–$5,000.

Food Festivals (chocolate, strawberries, shrimp, restaurants)

Celebrations of any local specialty can form the basis of a food festival. Ask area service groups or local restaurants to serve a special dish or two. Charge each group for its booth. People purchase tickets then trade them in for food. The charity gets a percentage of the money raised. Manpower: moderate. Staff is needed to line up vendors, for promotion, and to monitor the site the day of the event. Planning time: three to four months. Earning potential: $2,000–$40,000.

Home Tours (historical/neighborhood tours)

Arrange for a group of homes to be open to the public. They could be historic homes or several homes in one interesting neighborhood. The biggest obstacle to success is having to convince people to let crowds traipse through their homes. Manpower: high (security needed in each home). Planning time: three months. Earning potential: $500–$10,000.

Designer homes are more complicated. These generally involve an empty house (usually up for sale) and a number of interior designers, each decorating one room. Ticket prices are higher than for the home tours mentioned above. These take a lot of planning and coordination and can lose money. Boost revenue with fashion shows, luncheons at the home. Manpower: high. Planning time: six months to one year. Earning potential: $500–$10,000.

Jail

You can "arrest" local personalities and have them telephone friends to "post bail." Advertise heavily on radio and television so that people will call to turn in their friends for arrest. Manpower: moderate. You need a lot of drivers going out to arrest people and a bank of phones for the bail-out calls. Planning time: three months. Earning potential: $500–$10,000.

Mystery Night or Hunt

These can be simple or complex, depending on your initiative. There are professional companies that produce these and, unless you know how to do it yourself, hiring them can pay off. There are many site options here: a downtown area of a city, shopping center, amusement park, empty building, estate, or farm would all work well. Businesses might sponsor locations of the items on the route, refreshment stands, T-shirts. These are very popular now and are good ways to get people involved. Manpower: high. A lot of people are needed during the event. Planning time: three to four months. This is the sort of activity that tends to grow over time. Most only break even the first year they are held. Earning potential: $250–$10,000.

Nonevents

Send out cards inviting people to donate money without actually attending an event. Contributors save the expense of formal attire, gasoline, and babysitters. This can be a welcome change of pace for a charity that has a well-established group of contributors and perhaps has had a big, expensive event annually for some time. This is not a good first-time event because, as a fledgling or lesser-known charity, you aren't going to generate enough attention and name recognition to collect much money. Manpower: minimal. Planning time: six to eight weeks. Earning potential: $500–$10,000.

Opening Night

Like concerts, how much you make and how much work you have to do depends on whether you sponsor the performance yourself, or buy a block of tickets to someone else's performance. The former is more expensive, riskier, and requires more people than the latter. Earning potential: $150–$10,000.

Pancake Breakfast

Planning this event takes a week or less. Do invitations by phone or sign in front of fire station or by fliers. This is a low-cost, low-maintenance event, but it will also be low profit unless it is tied to something else like a raffle, giveaway, door prize, pass the basket. Such an event is more a "friend raiser." Earning potential: $100–$750.

Phonathon

Enlist a company to give you a room furnished with a number of desks and telephones. Have volunteers call people and solicit donations. This is a very successful means of making money for schools. You can make a lot of money from those who don't give on a regular basis or encourage regular donors to give more. To do this effectively, you need a lot of volunteers, a lot of phones, people to make calls during the days and others to phone people in the evenings. It helps to build incentives for your volunteers, awarding prizes to those who solicit the most money. Not much up-front money required, unless you have to rent an office and phones. Lead time: three to six months. Earning potential: $500–$2 million.

Raffle

Sell tickets to win something. You need to make sure it's legal in your community. (Some groups call this a "special prize program" to circumvent legal problems in areas where raffles are not permitted.) The better the prizes and odds of winning them, the more tickets will sell. Manpower: varies. Some will be needed to round up prizes, a larger number will be needed to sell tickets. With high-ticket items (such as cars), it's possible to sell a limited number of tickets at a higher price (i.e., 500 tickets at $1,000 each to win a Rolls Royce are likely to sell because the odds of winning will be greater than if 2,000 lesser-priced tickets were sold). Costs: minimal (printing of tickets). Don't conduct your raffle by mail. It's much more effective when your volunteers work face to face, as close to the actual drawing date as possible. Manpower: moderate. Earning potential: $500–$50,000.

Sidewalk Sale

Get volunteers to sell candy, baked goods, rummage items, plants, or crafts. This is an excellent first-time event because it gets people involved and builds a constituency. Volunteers can produce items at home, or collect them from garages and attics. The keys to success are a good location, enough people bringing in items, and proper promotion (newspaper, radio tie-in, fliers). Lead time: one month. While not likely to raise large amounts of money at a single sale, this event can be a solid revenue source if done on a regular basis. Earning potential: $500–$2,500.

Telethon/Radiothon

Telethons require tremendous resources in terms of manpower and staff. You need a bank of telephones, television time, people to handle the phones, and publicity. Generally, you need a professional producer to handle it. In all, you can quickly spend $400,000 before any money comes in. Planning time: six months to a year. Earning potential: $1,000–$8 million (Jerry Lewis's Muscular Dystrophy Telethon has earned the maximum).

Themed Meal (fashion show/luncheon, luau/dinner).

Pick a workable, attractive site, stick to your budget, and get whatever you can donated. Try to tie in a great door prize that fits the theme. Create an invitation and posters, organize committees and mailing lists to sell tickets and invite people. Manpower: moderate to high. These take lots of manpower, staff, and/or volunteer time. Planning time: four to six months. Earning potential: $250–$15,000.

Tournaments

Golf, tennis, and car-racing competitions are among the most popular tournaments used for fund raising. A successful tournament requires a lot of workers to line up sponsors and a site and promote the event. Up-front expenses are likely to be much greater than for most events because of deposits required for the site, printing, and sponsor information packages. Lead time: four to six months. The more sponsors, celebrities, and media time you can get, the more you are likely to make. Earning potential: $3,000–$70,000.

After developing your own list of possible events, figure out how many people might be required to carry them out successfully.

Start at the beginning: What do you need to do to get people to come? First you need to reserve a place to hold the event and set ticket/participation prices. Then invitations and/or press releases need to be printed and distributed. Then walk step-by-step through the planning and execution of the event. Once you know what the job entails, you will know how many people will be needed to do it.

Next, determine how many people you will be able to count on to help. While figuring that out, you will need to analyze the type of people who will be involved. Do they work outside the home on a full- or part-time basis? Do they have young children? If so, the amount of time they can devote to the event may be limited. (For details on committees, see chapter 4.)

It is vital to consider your own time in developing and producing an event. If you are a development officer or professional fund raiser, an event could consume half your time over a six-month period. If you have an active committee and chairman, your time commitment might not be as great. It is important to look at the big picture and decide how much of your time will be needed to raise a lot of money with an event. It might be more advantageous to pick up the phone and ask several corporations or wealthy patrons for large donations.

Next, consider how much money you have available to lay out for expenses. Even if you plan to take on something as seemingly simple as a spaghetti dinner, there are up-front costs to consider. You have to buy the spaghetti—and the rest of the food and beverages. If your group doesn't have them, you will need to rent tables and chairs, plates, cutlery. Then there's the site itself to pay for. Tickets and promotional materials have to be printed.

Just to give you an idea of how quickly expenses mount, let's take a look at a sample budget for a spaghetti dinner for 100 people:

SAMPLE BUDGET: SPAGHETTI DINNER FOR 100

Site rental (VFW Hall)	$100.00
Pasta (20 boxes @ 90 cents)	18.00
Sauce (canned tomatoes and seasonings)	50.00
Chopped meat for meatballs (20 lbs. at $1.70)	34.00
Beverages (soda, coffee, tea, wine)	67.00
Salad (lettuce, vegetables, dressing)	30.00
Bread (10 loaves)	10.00
Butter (2 pounds)	4.00
Dessert (ice cream, cookies)	25.00
Paper goods (150 plates, cups, napkins)	20.00
Plastic utensils	15.00
Plastic table cloths	5.00
Tables and chairs provided	—
Staff—volunteers	—
Pots and pans—donated	—
Printing—donated	—
TOTAL	378.00

Cost of meal per person	$ 3.78
Charge per person	$ 10.00
Profit per person	$ 6.22
Charity should make	$622.00

Once you have a ballpark idea of available staff and funds (for a step-by-step guide to calculating your budget, see chapter 2), the next thing to think about is how much lead time you have. You may be able to pull off a simple event in three months or so, but something like an auction or dinner/dance will require far more planning.

If you are thinking about changing the types of events the group has had, perhaps expanding from small events to those for which people will pay $150 or more a couple, you have to choose something that warrants the price—a dinner/dance cruise or concert with a big-name star, for example. If the attendees have a good time, they are likely to become long-term supporters.

Take a look at what types of events have been successful in your community. Even those that haven't been primarily fund raisers can sometimes be altered so that they do raise money.

The Miami Grand Prix Gala is an example of this. Since it began in 1983, it's become one of the most successful fund raisers in that city, despite the fact that it takes place at the end of the social season, following dozens of other such events. People buy tickets well in advance because it routinely sells out.

What makes it a perennial winner is that it attracts spectators 'from all over the world, giving it an international flavor. It features race-car drivers, who have a romantic allure. And the race itself is accessible to everyone because it takes place on the streets of downtown Miami.

The gala began as a simple cocktail reception to welcome the drivers, racing dignitaries, and corporate sponsors. It was a natural mix with which to launch an effective fund raiser. A local charity was chosen as the recipient for a three-year period, giving the charity the chance to build interest and attendance. The charity provides volunteers, front money, location, and theme, while the Grand Prix provides access to corporate sponsors and race-car drivers as well as the general allure of the event.

The nature of the gala changes annually. One year, it featured Roberta Flack in concert. Another year, it was a Great Gatsby theme party on the lavish grounds of the historic Vizcaya estate. It's an excellent example of how you can create a successful fund raiser by tying in to an already established local event.

Remember that raising money is the primary goal. If there is no existing event to which you can tie your charitable fund raiser, consider holding an event that has already proven successful in your area. If an event normally sells 3,000 seats at regular prices, you can likely sell 300 at the substantially higher rates you will have to charge to raise money.

Take into account all of your expenses, plus a bit more for unexpected items. Organizations that set standards for charities maintain that a properly handled fund raiser is one in which the charity gets 60 percent of the proceeds, with 40 percent or less used for expenses. While there is no law that requires such a standard, public opinion can be just as effective an enforcer.

Take, for example, the flap that arose in 1988 over a fund raiser for UNICEF and a new charity called the Creo Fund for Children with AIDS. In the hallowed halls of the United Nations Assembly, a cast of 150 performed the '60s musical *Hair* for a society-studded audience, each of whom paid $250 to $5,000 to attend.

Although contributions totaled $1 million, just $72,000 (less than 10 percent) actually got to the two charities, rather than the $600,000 that had been anticipated. The resulting criticism from disillusioned patrons prompted an investigation by the New York State Attorney General and the New York Philanthropic Advisory Service. Not only didn't the charity derive the financial benefit it had anticipated, but the resulting bad publicity is likely to have a negative impact on other donations for years to come.

One way to ensure that the charity gets the most from your fund-raising efforts is to enlist the financial help of area businesses. Keep an eye out for large businesses, such as department stores and hotels, that are preparing to open. Often they will be willing to host a charitable event as a promotion to help attract big spenders. Besides providing the location, they may pay for invitations and food. All the charity has to do is bring in the monied people that both it and the business want to attract.

TIP: Always be prepared to let contributors know exactly how much of what they pay is a tax-deductible donation to the charity and how much goes to expenses.

Time and Date

You can plan the best event of the social season, design it exactly right for your target audience, have access to unlimited funds and manpower, and still have a flop if you schedule it wrong.

Most communities have some sort of social calendar or events schedule. Check with the chamber of commerce and tourism offices and, if a schedule exists, make sure the date you are considering is not crammed with several other popular events.

If no central calendar exists, check with places likely to host major events—convention centers, big hotels, and any other places capable of holding a large gathering. Also check with major churches to see if a religious holiday conflicts with your planned date. In a college town, make sure there isn't a big game or homecoming that day. Check with the newspaper to see if its events file lists any events for that date.

If you plan an outdoor event, consult weather experts for the likelihood of bad weather. *The Farmer's Almanac* and the weather bureau are good sources, too. You will want to inquire about weather on that date in previous years. Depending on where you live, you might want to consider the effect of a possible tornado, hurricane, or snowstorm. Obviously, even thorough groundwork cannot ward off an act of nature, but you improve your odds this way.

Think about what happens when in your community, too. In Florida, for example, an outdoor event in August is likely to fail. Aside from the brutal heat and humidity, the bulk of part-time residents as well as tourists are up north. By holding events during the winter, the traditional social season, southern charities reap the benefit of a larger population from which to attract attendance. The reverse is true in the North. You would not want to plan a big event in Newport in January because the weather is nasty and most of the wealthy summer residents have headed south.

Besides the time of year, there are better and worse times of the week to hold events. Previews and other small events are best held right after work on a Tuesday or Thursday evening before people go home. If you are planning a Friday night event, schedule it late enough so that people have time to go home, get changed, and get back for the event. On a Sunday, events should be scheduled early enough for people to get home and prepare for work on Monday.

This is one of the trickiest aspects of scheduling. You might think you have a great event scheduled for an ideal time. You might be wrong. Consider the following case:

The University of Miami/Jackson Memorial Burn Center planned a Saturday lunch on a cruise ship that would be in port that day. The Costa Cruise Line donated the use of the ship and a catered lunch for up to 200 people. The cruise line also helped pay for the invitations.

It sounded like a good idea. The charity would get an event at virtually no cost while the cruise line would get to show off its ship to monied people likely to book future cruises.

But when only ten replies came back from a mailing of 500 invitations, the event organizer started asking around to see what the problem was. It turned out that Saturdays were when many people planned family activities. The luncheon was canceled, but it wasn't a total loss. The cruise line generously donated a cruise the charity could auction off to raise money at a later event.

Where you have an event is as important as when. If you expect 50 people to turn up, don't rent a hall that holds 500. A room that holds 50 is going to be unsuitable if an extra 20 people show up (more in chapter 5).

Before you make a commitment to do a special event, be sure you have the resources—in manpower and money—to make it enjoyable and financially successful. Read on for ways to ensure this.

CHECKLIST

Purpose of the Event

- ☐ Primarily to raise money
- ☐ Gain new members, new donors
- ☐ Get publicity and/or visibility

Determine Your Target Audience

- ☐ Whom are you trying to reach?
- ☐ How many people do you want to attend?
- ☐ How many people are required to make the event a success?
- ☐ Where will your audience come from? What are they willing to spend?
- ☐ Is the event something people might attend if it were not for charity?

Program Event Ideas

- ☐ Will it help achieve your group's goals?
- ☐ Will it interest the audience at which the event is aimed?
- ☐ Do you have enough time to plan this event?
- ☐ Do you have enough staff/volunteer support?
- ☐ Can you afford to stage such an event?
- ☐ Is an appropriate and affordable site available?
- ☐ Has this type of event been successful before?
- ☐ Are there potential corporate sponsors?

Check the Calendar

- ☐ Did you make sure there are no conflicts with other major events?

☐ Have you checked the weather on that date for the past few years?

☐ Did you set your day and time to fit the audience's work schedule?

Chapter 2

Money Matters

A charity event should be run just like any other business: You need to know what the up-front costs are, that there is sufficient capital to cover them, and enough personnel are available to make it happen. Just as in setting up a business, the goal is to make money. Consequently, you have to draw up a plan and do careful research before committing to the event. An event, especially a big one, can cost a lot, often more than the organization has on hand. While the event might end up raising a lot of money, if costs get out of control or you are unable to sell enough tickets, financial ruin can result. By figuring out costs first, you can determine whether you can afford to have the event and what the chances are of making money on it. Sometimes it's better to decide *not* to hold an event, rather than risk destroying the organization with a financially diastrous one.

First take a look at Figure 2-1, which depicts a budget worksheet. It gives you the basic factors you need to consider when determining what an event will cost. Before you spend anything, you have to know what your budgetary limits are.

How much can you afford to spend on an event? Start by looking at how much your group has in the bank. Subtract from

Figure 2-1. Budget Worksheet

EXPENSES

Space rentals

Additional site costs
    Box office
    Lighting
    Audio/Visual
    Subtotal

Food and catering
    Food _____ persons @ _____
    per person
    Equipment rental
    Gratuities (18 percent)
    Subtotal

Entertainment
    Music
    Talent
    Honoraria
    Transportation
    Subtotal

Decorations

Security

Insurance

Graphics (design, typography, printing, etc.)
    Invitations
    Ad book/program
    Tickets
    Media kits
    Posters
    Signs
    Prizes, plaques, certificates
    Subtotal

Publicity
    Publicist
    Photographer
    Reproduction, mailing services, etc.
    Media advertising
    Entertaining and free tickets
    Phone bills
    Subtotal

Postage
    Invitations
    Tickets
    Publicity
    Subtotal

Special events production firm

Miscellaneous (specialized) costs

Add 20 percent contingency fund

Projected Financial Data Worksheet

INCOME				SUBTOTALS

Seating and sponsorship of $_____ per seat/ticket _____ seats.
Additional Sponsorship

Levels		Purchaser Receives	Projected Sales	Additional Income
Benefactors	$____	____ seats	____	$____
Patrons	$____	____ / tickets	____	$____
Sponsors	$____	____ seats	____	$____
Contributors	$____	____ seats	____	$____
Raffle	$____	____ ticket	____	$____
Cash Bar	$____	____ ticket/drink	____	$____

AD/Program Book

Levels		Purchaser Receives		Projected Sales	Additional Income
Benefactors	$____	____ page	____ tickets	____	$____
Patrons	$____	____ page	____ tickets	____	$____
Sponsors	$____	____ page	____ tickets	____	$____
Contributors	$____	____ page	____ tickets	____	$____
Listing	$____	____ page	____ tickets	____	$____

TOTAL ANTICIPATED INCOME _____
TOTAL PROJECTED EXPENSES _____
PROJECTED NET PROFIT [LOSS] _____

that the amount you'll need to keep the group operating for at least two months (three is better). Whatever is left over is the amount you can afford to lose. Of course, you aren't setting out to lose it, but if the worst happens, the organization can continue to function.

For example, if your group has $3,000 in the bank and it costs $1,000 a month to run, you have $1,000 left to wager on an event. This means a $50,000 event is out of your price range (unless you line up some major corporate sponsors to cover the other $49,000—more on that later in the chapter).

If you don't have enough money to launch the event you want to produce, consider linking up with another charity and splitting the costs and the profits. In doing this, however, be specific about who does what and what each group's financial obligations will be. Write it all down and sign it. (See figure 2-2 for a sample agreement letter.)

Approach it the way you would the purchase of a house; if you use up all your money buying the house, you won't have any left to

Figure 2-2. Sample Agreement Letter

MIAMI SHORE THEATER OF PERFORMING ARTS
Miami Shores, Florida

Mr. Harry Freedman
UM/JM Burn Center
P. O. Box 016310
Miami, Florida 33101

Dear Harry:

This letter is to confirm the topics discussed at our last meeting with you representing the UM/JM Burn Center, and Connie Willman and myself representing the Miami Shores Theater of Performing Arts.

We look forward to working with you together on the upcoming "Spring Fashion Show" which will be held on Thursday, March 15, 1990 at the Sheraton Bal Harbour. Cocktails will begin at 11:30 a.m. followed by lunch at 12:00 noon with a fashion show being held at 12:30 P.M. The cost of each seat will be $50.00.

All expenses will be paid from the proceeds of the event and the net amount will be divided equally (50/50) between the UM/JM Burn Center and the Miami Shores Theater of Performing Arts each party will provide $1,000 to cover advanced expenses such as printing, postage and hotel deposit.

Please sign and return this letter as an indication of your acceptance of this agreement between both parties.

We look forward to working with you on this exciting event.

Sincerely,   Agreed to:_____

Terry Schechter

Terry Schechter   Harry A. Freedman, Director of Development
Miami Shores Theater of   UM/JM Burn Center
Performing Arts
                                                    Date:__Sept 21, 1990__

---

live on. Just as you don't want to be house poor, you don't want to be special events poor, either.

Once you've determined what you have available to spend, you then have to figure out your costs and how much your organization can afford to lay out before any money comes in. A budget also helps prevent haphazard spending, which can mount quickly, and ensure you make the greatest profit possible.

Location

After you've decided what kind of event you would like to have (see chapter 1), you have to determine where you will hold it. Location will play a major role in determining what your event will cost. (See chapter 5 for a full discussion of locations.)

A hotel may seem expensive at first, but remember that many costs are included in the price. Hotels usually provide a ballroom; rooms for changing, storage, and meetings; cocktail hour space; and terrace areas all for the cost of the food. Not included are such things as staging, lighting, decorations, special effects, marching elephants, or anything out of the ordinary. And some hotels are not equipped to provide the electrical and loading facilities needed to handle large-scale stage shows.

The opening of the Miami Hilton was a gala event, but its organizers will best remember it for the difficulty they had in finding a portable stage and adequate lights and sound systems less than a week before the event. Owner Barron Hilton underwrote the entertainment, which featured Rita Moreno and David Brenner. The lighting and sound requirements for their Las Vegas–style shows were extensive. Most hotels, the Miami Hilton included, don't have a stage large enough to accommodate such shows, so one had to be borrowed from another hotel. Then there was the lighting. The hotel manager was less than thrilled watching the sound and light people drill holes in his brand new ceiling to hang the lights.

Convention hotels—with big ballrooms and meeting spaces—are ideal for larger-scale events and can more easily accommodate big stage shows. Of course, they generally cost more, too.

Hotels often provide a list of the cost of additional services, personnel, and equipment, and many have audiovisual consultants either in house or under contract. Figure 2-3 shows a contract with an audiovisual company. Shop around and compare prices. Hotels across the street from one another may have vastly different costs and, as a result, widely ranging charges. When inquiring about prices, make sure you indicate how many rooms you'll need for volunteers, celebrities, and set-up crews.

TIP: You can often get free rooms thrown in if the catering department is not willing to give you a break on the price of food. Many hotels provide free rooms for celebrities in exchange for photos of the stars at the hotel.

Public Buildings

Many public buildings can prove interesting spots for special events. City hall courtyards, stock exchanges, museums, cultural halls, government meeting rooms or school auditoriums are all possibilities. First, find out what it costs to use the room and whether there are any restrictions on its use. Some public buildings can be reserved without charge, but be aware of conditions that can mount expenses quickly. Many such buildings have no kitchen, dishes, glasses, tableclothes, or an adequate supply of chairs. In many cases, you'll need to hire security guards and possibly a clean-up crew. There are even places that require you to bring in your own garbage bags to haul off debris.

In Philadelphia, a day-care facility was offered the use of the top floor of a spectacular office building, the Penn Mutual Towers, for a fund-raising fashion show and buffet dinner. The huge open space seemed the perfect setting. But a month before the event, the caterer called to say the building's small kitchen was inadequate to feed 400 people. He would need to bring in ovens and an array of kitchen equipment. That was in addition to the charity having to supply tables, tableclothes, dishes, silverware, pots and pans, and napkins, chairs, fans, waiters, and a runway for the fashion show.

Figure 2-3. Audiovisual Contract

Proposal Page No. of Pages

SOUTHERN AUDIO VISUAL
PGA Sheraton Resort
400 Avenue of the Champions
PALM BEACH GARDENS, FLORIDA 33410
(305) 622-7404

PROPOSAL SUBMITTED TO: Parkinson Foundation		PHONE	DATE: February 14, 1984
STREET: 1501 N.W. 9th Avenue		JOB NAME: Lionel Hampton/Phyllis Diller Show	
CITY, STATE AND ZIP CODE: Miami, FL 33136		JOB LOCATION: The Breakers Hotel - 2/27/84	
ARCHITECT: Bruce Sutka	DATE OF PLANS: 2/14/84		JOB PHONE

We hereby submit specifications and estimates for:

4 - Yamaha 15" Cabinets, Main sound system
4 - 1218 Altec speakers, Main sound system
2 - 15" JBL Cabinets, Main sound system
5 - Crown 500 amplifiers
4 - Monitor wedges (Yamaha)
1 - Peavey XR600 monitor amplifier
15 - Wired microphones, cables and stands
1 - Backup wireless amplifier

Scaffolding
Drapes

2 - Men to set-up and dismantle
1 - Man to operate

TOTAL 1,643.00

We Propose hereby to furnish material and labor — complete in accordance with above specifications, for the sum of:

One thousand six hundred forty three and 00/100------------------- dollars ($ 1,643.00).

Payment to be made as follows:

In full within 15 days of billing date.

All material is guaranteed to be as specified. All work to be completed in a workmanlike manner according to standard practices. Any alteration or deviation from above specifications involving extra costs will be executed only upon written orders, and will become an extra charge over and above the estimate. All agreements contingent upon strikes, accidents or delays beyond our control. Owner to carry fire, tornado and other necessary insurance. Our workers are fully covered by Workmen's Compensation Insurance.

Authorized Signature ____ Jan Thigpen, Vice President

Note: This proposal may be withdrawn by us if not accepted within 7 days.

Acceptance of Proposal — The above prices, specifications and conditions are satisfactory and are hereby accepted. You are authorized to do the work as specified. Payment will be made as outlined above.

Signature ____

Date of Acceptance: ____

Signature ____

FORM 118-3 COPYRIGHT 1960 - Available from NEBS Inc. Groton, Mass. 01450

Because the penthouse had a glass dome top, there were strict regulations about the installation of decorations, lighting, and sound equipment.

Many of these items had not been budgeted for, but the ticket prices had long since been set. The choice now was to either have a cold meal or bring in all the equipment to do it right. The charity opted for the latter, which cut deeply into the money it expected to raise. The site was truly spectacular, but the same effect could have been created in a hotel ballroom and the charity would have netted another $20,000.

Other Buildings

There are many other options for event sites. In most communities service and fraternal organizations have their own buildings. With some creative decorating and good food, an organization can stage a fine event while keeping costs low.

Outdoor Locations

Outdoor sites, such as parks and beaches, are attractive spots for special events because, in addition to their natural beauty, they often have unlimited space and the advantage of being able to accommodate several activities at once. Municipal parks, zoos, botanical gardens, and beaches are among the most commonly used outdoor sites.

Before committing to an outdoor site, check the costs for licensing and cleanup. If you expect to serve alcohol, check to make sure it's legal. Also determine whether you can require everyone to pay admission and if you can exclude those who are not invited to the event. When the University of Miami Burn Center used a public beach for a fund-raising party, it was not permitted to charge admission. Instead, the hospital held a raffle. For $3, people bought a chance to win airline tickets to anywhere in the United States.

You might also consider holding a raffle for a car or cruise. But keep in mind that not everyone will want to buy tickets and you cannot require them to in such cases. Sometimes you can close a public facility, but it takes a lot of paperwork, time, and often, political pull.

Some other expenses you might incur at outdoor spots include security and emergency medical personnel.

Churches and synagogues

Churches and synagogues are well suited to concerts. However, if you plan to serve food, check whether there are restrictions on what food or beverages can be served there. Churches and synagogues also generally restrict the days and times they can be rented. The biggest advantage to churches is that the large sanctuaries already are equipped with seating and light and sound systems, things that must be set up in auditoriums or hotel ballrooms. And most also have an area in which a simple reception may be held. All this, of course, saves on expenses and maximizes your profit. Composer/pianist Marvin Hamlisch frequently performs in synagogues, setting up his piano on the pulpit. The Vienna Boys Choir often performs in church cathedrals.

Audiovisual and Lighting

Lighting and sound can be very simple—a single mike with portable public address system and a spotlight. But if the lighting and sound do not suit the event, it will flop. What is worse than having a speaker you can't hear, a singer whose voice is drowned out by the screech of a malfunctioning microphone, or a play in which the actors look like shadows among the props? There's one sure way to guard against this type of disaster, budget enough money to hire pros. In this area more than many others, you truly get what you pay for. No matter how good cousin Eddie was at wiring Uncle Mort's stereo, don't let him set up the sound for your event. Shop around for a professional, taking with you a list of what the performers require (see chapter 6). Prices can vary widely for this.

TIP: There are often different rates for commercial and charity jobs. Ask.

Food and Catering

How glamorous does it have to be? Food should be edible, presented in an attractive manner, and not so expensive that the charity ends up breaking even or, worse, losing money. Usually food is among the biggest expenses. If money is tight, opt for an unusual light menu rather than having an extensive meal with rubber chicken. Consider serving a smaller meal, then finishing with a sumptuous dessert buffet (see chapter 7).

Another large expense is liquor, if you choose to serve it. Many hotels require that you use their liquor service and charge on a per drink or per bottle basis. There can also be a corkage charge—even if the wine and champagne are donated—which can run as much as $10 a bottle. Ask ahead. It's very easy to have your per person liquor costs equal the rest of the meal.

The best way to save on food and beverages is to get someone to underwrite them. A prime example of how this can be done successfully was the 1989 Grand Prix Gala in Miami, which was to benefit the Miami Burn Center and Mailman Child Development Center. Rather than having the usual sit-down dinner, the group opted for buffet–style international dining galleries. There were three areas from which the 600 guests could choose food: Oriental (underwritten by Nissan); European, mainly French and Italian (underwritten by Martini and Rossi); and Miami cuisine, a mix of hamburgers, pizza, hot dogs, Cuban, Jewish, Haitian, and Bahamian food (underwritten by BellSouth Mobility, a cellular phone company). Figure 2-4 is a sample menu proposal.

Figure 2-4. Sample Menu Proposal

OMNI INTERNATIONAL HOTEL

January 16, 1989

JoAnn Ryburn
Miami Motor Sports
7254 S.W. 48th St.
Miami, Florida 33155

Dear JoAnn,

As per my conversation with Harry Friedman on Monday, January
9, 1989, regarding the March 3, 1989, Grand Prix Gala, the
following menu was suggested:

In separate areas of our Ballroom level three theme oriented
buffets will be created.

The first, an Oriental area will consist of : Sushi and
Sashimi, Chinese Chicken Salad, Mini Egg Rolls, Vegetable
Tempura, Fried Wontons, Shrimp Fried Rice, Sweet and Sour
Pork, Snow Peas with Water Chestnuts and Baby Corn, Almond
Cookies and Fortune Cookies.

The second buffet area will be a Miami Style/Latin Creole/
Jewish American one, consisting of the following: (3) carving
stations, with chefs slicing Top Rounds of Beef Au Jus, Whole
Tom Turkeys with stuffing and Cranberry Sauce, and Whole
Baked Hams. All with the appropriate condiments and split
rolls. Black Beans and Rice, Fried Plantains, Jalapeno
Potato Salad, Chilled Gaspacho Soup, Assorted Pizzas with
varied toppings, mini-bagels with sliced Salmon, Onions,
Tomatoes and Cream Cheese, Conch Salad, Fresh Island Fruit
Kabobs, Corn and Banana Breads, Cucumber Salad and Carrot
and Raisin Salad.

Con't/d

Miami Motor Sports
Page II

The third area will be a European Buffet area, consisting
of:
Pasta Stations with chefs preparing Tortellini and Fettucine
with (2) different sauces, Deluxe Antipasto, Hot and Spicy
Italian Sausage, Cold Vegetable and Pasta Salad, Caesar Salad
prepared to order, Scallops in puffed pastry, Fried Mozzarella,
Prosciutto Ham with Melon, Mini Veal Parmessan, Vegetable
Ravioli, Italian Bread and Butter.

In addition to the above, the Omni will provide desserts
and Coffee so that each dinner table of (10) will become
its own Mini Vienese table complete with a wonderful varied
selection of Cakes and Pies, Petite Fours, Chocolate Covered
Fruits, Cookies and Candies. The hotel will also provide
individual cordial trays for each table complete with Whipped
Cream, Cinnamon and Chocolate Bits.

JoAnn, I am very excited about this function and look forward
to a wonderful evening. It is also my understanding now
that we have a budget of $60,000.00 based on 900 people.

JoAnn, thank you for your help. Should you have any
questions, please do not hesitate to call.

Sincerely,

David Kurland
Director of Catering

DK/jc

cc: Mr. Harry Friedman

In return for underwriting one dining gallery, each company got two tables at the event for its executives, banners with its name in each gallery, and recognition in the program book. Martini and Rossi supplied wines and champagne, the only liquors served that night. The only food for which the charity paid was the dessert buffet provided by the hotel for $12 a person. Because costs were kept so low, the charity could afford to bring in singer Roberta Flack for a concert following the dinner.

Even when you can't get the whole menu underwritten, you might be able to get local businesses to agree to underwrite portions, such as the cocktail hour. If you have ample hors d'oeuvres and drinks, the meal need not be as large or lavish.

Food costs at hotels are absolutely negotiable. Send in a strong negotiator to handle this job. Just because you are quoted $18.50 per person for Chicken à la Hotel doesn't mean you can't get the price reduced by 20 or 30 percent. Suggest that the dish be modified to make it less expensive.

In most towns, hotels are highly competitive. If you're bringing in one of the season's bigger events, they will want your business. If you have a celebrity in tow, your bargaining position is even stronger. Push for everything you can get.

Hotels require that you guarantee that a certain number of people will attend. That's how they determine which ballroom to use, how much food to buy, and how much staff will be needed.

TIP: Be careful of the guarantee. A week before the event, guarantee 20 percent fewer people than you have collected money from. When you give the final guarantee—48 hours before the event—make sure it's in writing.

If you guarantee 300 people and only 200 show, you pay for the full 300. Don't worry about having enough food if you guarantee fewer than actually show up—hotels always prepare 15 percent more than the guarantee.

If you are holding the event somewhere other than a hotel, your organization or the caterer must secure the equipment needed. Caterers generally will do this, adding 15 to 20 percent to the price of renting such things as chairs, tables, etc., for providing the service. If your group has a capable person who can handle this job, you can save quite a bit of money. Most communities have rental companies that can supply the items you need. Make sure the person handling the job understands the intricacies of what is needed to prepare and serve a meal. He or she should consult with the caterer before renting equipment.

TIP: Don't forget to budget for gratuities—the customary rate is 18 percent.

Feeding Staff and Help

When volunteers work all day setting up the site, and you have other paid individuals, such as sound and light crew, musicians, etc., you may have to feed them lunch and/or dinner before the event. Be sure you know in advance what's required—sandwiches or pizza and soft drinks. See if a fast-food company will provide this in return for advertising or publicity. Make sure the hotel will allow you to bring in food from outside; some try to prevent this. Insist upon it, especially if you are staging a big, costly event.

TIP: The one item you almost always have to buy from the hotel is coffee service. Concede graciously.

Entertainment

As important as serving palatable food is making sure people have fun. That's entertainment. If your budget is tight, the best entertainment is the kind that is donated. If you can't get it donated, you have to buy it. The more complicated the entertainment, the more expensive it becomes—sound, light, production costs, staging, and technical staff are among the things that will cost money. When you hire big-time celebrities, the costs are guaranteed to escalate on every front (see chapter 6).

TIP: Some entertainers require certain brands of instruments. Try to get them donated by the local distributor in exchange for publicity. Your local piano store may provide the piano—and sometimes a pianist— for an event, in return for mention in promotional material.

Remember to budget for honoraria that may be required for the entertainer as well as any transportation he or she may require (airplanes and limousines, for instance), hotel rooms, and meals. The entertainer's contracts will list these requirements.

Decorations

Many people go overboard on decorations. This is an excellent aspect in which to involve businesses or individuals in underwriting and donation.

If you can afford to hire a party planner, you might be able to create a more stylish ambiance, not to mention the advantage of one less responsibility you and your staff must handle. In terms of cost, using party planners may be no more expensive than purchasing a lot of elaborate decorations. The planner is apt to have on hand a selection of props and supplies you might otherwise be unable to find or afford (see figure 2-5).

TIP: A party planner will sometimes donate work if it provides good advertising for his or her services. You might try to convince a planner to donate the work for all or part of one event in exchange for a larger, paying event.

Security

Security is important to control crowds, protect your guests and facilities, and keep out gate-crashers. It's much easier for a uniformed security person to deal with a people problem than it is for one of your tuxedo-clad committee members. A guest who may

Figure 2-5. Sample Party Planners Bid

PROPOSAL FOR GRAND PRIX GALA 1989 OMNI HOTEL

FROM: PARTY PRODUCTIONS, MIAMI, FLORIDA

International decor to consist of as follows:

Travel to the Orient and find our beautiful Oriental props specially designed around food areas which includes our realistic Sushi screens, elaborate giant Pandas nestled in bamboo, Kabuki characters and large bamboo planters for added decor and entrance. Black, gold, red and white fabric and flowers will be used to enhance buffet tables and props. Urns with exotic florals and a spectacular pagoda make you even more convinced you're not in Miami any more...

Our next stop is Europe where you will find an Italian Villa with trimmed trees and plants, balustrades, columns and urns with flowers like Rome in the Spring. French doors and windows peer out upon an open air Cafe'. Umbrellas on tables, ferns and flowers give just the right hint of Paris.

As the Concorde lands you feel right at home on South Beach. Miami's Art Deco section comes to life as large Palms sway in the breeze against the pastel colored Skyline. Neon Palms and Flamingos, Beach Umbrellas, hot colored fabrics and wild "Deco" florals bring you back home.

BALLROOM:

> We'll provide eight black, white and red multi height cubes for each table to hold deserts. Fabric will be woven around cubes to soften the look.

RECEPTION:

> The reception area says, "Lets Race Around the World" with international flags and panels with racing posters.

Total special price for above mentioned decor...$7,500.00

We're looking forward to making this a most enjoyable occasion for you and your guests.

If this proposal meets with your approval, kindly sign below and return to our office. Balance due on render of services.

Sincerely,

Roni Harkey
Roni Harkey
PARTY PRODUCTIONS

Agreed to and Accepted by:

_____

Date:_ 2/20/89 _

RH/jb
Enclosures:

---

have had too much to drink (and who might also be a major contributor), is apt to more readily accept a ride home from a uniformed security guard than from a member of the board. As with everything, get estimates. Hire a private security company or check to see if off-duty police are available for hire in your community.

Insurance

Many facilities require you to purchase additional liability insurance to protect them and your organization against injuries that may befall guests. This also protects you in case someone working on props or sets gets injured. If you plan an outdoor event, consider buying weather insurance in case of inclement weather.

Graphics, Arts, Etc.

The first notice most people receive about your event is your hold-the-date postcard (so people can mark their calendars early in the social season) or the invitation, so these need to be eye-catching. Make sure the invitation is the proper size and weight for a standard envelope, unless you've budgeted for additional postage. Corporate logos can appear on the invitations in return for companies paying all or part of the printing costs. Many large companies have their own printing facilities or have contracts with printing companies and may be willing to have your invitations printed as part of a larger run. (Some have their own graphic artists who might design your invitations, too.)

Don't forget your other printing costs: media packets, posters, signage, tickets, certificates, plaques, ad books, and programs.

Again, it's important to shop around; get at least three bids on a printing job. And don't underorder. A smaller second run can sometimes cost as much or more than your initial run. Over and above the number you need to send to potential guests, add extras to send to the news media and to people on the committee members' personal lists (see chapter 4).

Sometimes you can trade with printers. The charity supplies a certain number of tickets to the event in exchange for recognition of the printer on all printed materials. When hiring a printer, make sure you check on all costs, including paper, ink, graphic design, folding, and assembly. Make sure he can get the job done on time, too. It doesn't help to have beautiful invitations if they arrive too late.

TIP: Save money by having someone do the layout (typesetting) on a home or office computer. The same can be done with fliers and posters.

Publicity

For proper publicity, certain printed materials are vital. Among them: press releases, appropriate photographs, and—possibly—ad space. Many newspapers have discounted rates for charities or will list your event in community calendars at no cost. (For more on news media, see chapter 8.) Other avenues of free publicity include placing posters in store windows, at hotel desks, and at the meeting places of social, civic, and religious groups.

Publicists and Photographers

For larger events, consider hiring a site publicist with specific tasks assigned for an agreed-upon price. This is often preferable to hiring someone to do publicity in general. You might also want to hire a photographer to document the event from the planning stages through the event itself. Again, get bids and references before hiring anyone.

Entertaining

There are times when you may have to take major committee members out for a meal while planning meetings. Occasionally, restaurants will donate a luncheon for a small group of committee members, especially if they are socially prominent.

Sometimes you can negotiate with hotels for a certain number of planning meetings with cake and coffee or lunch included, depending on how persuasive you are. Some hotels will allow you to bring a group of four to six people for a tasting of the menu items a month or so prior to the event. This is a great way to stimulate key committee people to sell tickets.

Free Tickets

The best policy is to avoid giving out free tickets. Invariably, you'll need to give some seats away, but it's best to find some means of paying for them. Large companies will often purchase blocks of tickets for their executives or favored clients to use. You might request that if they are unable to use them, the businesses notify you so that you may distribute them to the media or VIPs, making sure that you give credit to the donor companies that provided them.

Postage

When figuring out how much your postage will cost, make sure you include your publicity mailings as well as invitations. Add some extra to cover correspondence with the news media (including press kits), key committee people, solicitation of corporations, and mailing out tickets.

If you are mailing enough invitations—say 1,000 or more— you can save money by using bulk rate if you have enough lead time. The advantage is that it's about half the normal first-class rate. The drawbacks are that you must first sort it by ZIP code and it almost always takes longer to arrive.

Specialized Costs

Every event is different. You may need to add some special categories. A fashion show, for example, may include expenses such as dressers, racks for clothing, makeup and hairdressing, extended staging, and runways. See figure 2-6 for a list of specialized costs for a Special Olympics benefit. A food festival might require extensive tenting, booths, and electrical generators. For a guest speaker, you may need to pay an honorarium. If you have a big-name star, you'll probably need extra security as well as transportation and possibly a box office from which to sell tickets.

Special Events Planners

There are a number of people who can help you produce special events:

Party Planners

Party planners are paid to come up with the theme, decorations, talent, menu, and music. They usually charge a fee plus a 10 to 25 percent markup on all products and services.

Special Events Production Firms

A production firm usually handles larger-scale events that require outdoor staging, lights, gigantic projection screens, stadium seating, fireworks, and crowd control. They also normally come up with a theme and big-name celebrities. These firms usually work for a fee plus a percentage (15 to 23 percent) based on costs.

Fund-Raising Consultant

A fund-raising consultant looks at the event from a financial standpoint to make sure it will raise enough money and to keep expenses to a minimum. He or she often advises charities on creative ways to get underwriting and corporate sponsorships and how to increase attendance. Sometimes a consultant will direct the

Figure 2-6. Sample List of Specialized Costs

ADVANCE SHEET: SPECIAL OLYMPICS BENEFIT WITH THE 76er's WIVES AND ALBERT NIPON SHOW
7 APRIL 83   FRANKLIN PLAZA HOTEL, PHILADELPHIA

TASK	SCHEDULE	BLOOMIES	HOTEL	76er's DRG.	NIPON	OTHER
Backdrop						
Design/color/heigth/width/material	TBD					Mark Needle
Positioning	After erection of runway		X			
Backstage						
Rolling racks	By 3:00 pm	X				
Ironing boards/irons	By 3:00 pm	X				
Person to iron	By 5:00 pm				X	
Extension cords	By 4:00 pm	X				
Tables (6') for accessories (4)	By 4:00 pm		X			
Chairs (6)	By 4:00 pm		X			
Mirrors	By 4:00 pm	X				
Beverages (Perrier/white wine)	By 7:15 pm		X			
Lighting:total	By 3:00 pm		X			
Lighting						
spots (2)	By 5:30 pm for rehearsal		X			
non-blinking track for runway	By 5:30 pm				X	
operator for spots in booth	By 5:30 pm		X			
Props						
Flowers for Pearl Nipon	Presented by Turquoise Erving at conclusion of show	X				
Rehearsal						
Dressers.	By 4:45 pm	X				
Music	By 4:00 pm				X	
Runway						
Positioning (see attached chart)	By 3:00 pm or ASAP		X			
Covering (rug surface)	By 3:00 pm		X			
Securing and skirting (beige)	By 4:00 pm		X			
Sound						
All speakers in main ballroom "on"	By 5:30 pm for rehearsal		X			
All speakers in dressing room "off"	By 5:30 pm for rehearsal		X			
Three (3) headsets: 2 in booth;1 bkstg	By 5:30 pm for rehearsal		X	X		
Two (2) cassette machines in booth	By 5:00 pm for rehearsal		X	X		
Musical cassette. tapes	By 5:00 pm for rehearsal				X	
Microphone	By 5:30 pm for rehearsal		X			
Staffing						
Dressers: 16	By 4:45 pm	X				
Cosmeticians (Chanel;2 make-up artists) with materials	By 6:45 pm	X				
Hairdressers	By 6:30 pm				X	
Starters (Helen/Melissa)	By 7:15 pm				X	
Transportation						
Nipon stock/accessories	TBD				X	
All Bloomingdale's logistical support	TBD	X				
Wives Participation						
Appearance in show with Special Olympic children and player-husbands.	At start of show 7:45 pm	X		X	X	

Program of evening

6:30pm	Guests arrive. Cocktails commence.
	Silent auction commences.
7:30pm	Guests proceed to ballroom
7:45pm	Show commences
8:15pm	Show concludes
8:30pm	Dinner is served

ordering of invitations, devise the theme, and coordinate entertainment. These people normally work for a straight consulting fee.

If your event is a party aimed at getting publicity for your organization, a party planner will be suitable. If you are looking to raise money, you might want to use a professional fund raiser, who will likely hire the party planner as well as figure out how to get corporate underwriting. If it's a very large event, consider a special-events production firm and possibly a fund raiser to keep an eye on costs.

Setting Ticket Prices

After you have all the bids and can determine the cost of your proposed event, add another 20 percent to that figure as a contingency fund (no matter how experienced you are at staging events, unexpected expenses always crop up). Then look at the number of people you think you can easily attract. This is often the hardest figure to come up with. If committees are properly structured and their obligations regarding ticket sales are spelled out, you should be able to come up with a reasonably accurate number (see chapter 4). Take that number and divide it into the total expenses. This gives you the amount per person you will need to cover the costs of the event.

This is when you decide whether you are having a friend-raising event or a fund-raising event. You want the charity to get at least 60 percent of the money you bring in, so to create a comfortable cushion, double the figure you'll need to cover expenses. For example:

EXPENSE ESTIMATE FOR FASHION SHOW/LUNCHEON FOR 300 PEOPLE

Cost per person (food, printing, postage) $25
Fashion show—underwritten   —
Site rental—underwritten   —
Total cost $25 × 300 people   7,500

If ticket price is $50, charity nets	$7,500
If ticket price is $75, charity nets	$15,000
If ticket price is $100, charity nets	$22,500

Before determining the ticket price, check to see what other organizations charge for similar events. Make sure the price you ask isn't beyond the means or spending habits of the people you are trying to attract. This is where your previous marketing tests should pay off.

Again, remember to consider the worst case. You may expect 300 people to attend, but end up selling only 200 tickets. You might think you'll get the whole event underwritten, but find only half the expenses are covered. Before forging ahead, you must decide if it's worth spending three to six months to stage an event that won't generate the income you hoped for.

Underwriting

By most industry reckonings, some 3,500 corporations spend $2 billion to $3 billion a year on sponsorships and donations to nonprofit groups. That doesn't include the thousands of smaller businesses that also provide substantial support. By attracting corporate executives to your committees, you are in a better position to get a share of these dollars. Individuals in law firms, banks, and accounting firms may have clients who may be looking to get involved in such causes. Businesspeople like to see their names appear in connection with projects that serve the community. Sponsoring an event is a good way for a new business or corporate executive to make his or her name known.

When seeking corporate sponsorship, it's not enough to say your cause is a worthy one. There are thousands of those. Do your homework and be ready to sell your group. See the sample corporate solicitation letter in figure 2-7. Be prepared to tell company officials how many people you expect and their median age and income. Be able to tell the company what it will get for its contribution—i.e., banners at the event; a listing in advertising, on the invitations, and in the program book; exposure in radio and

Figure 2-7. Sample Corporate Solicitation Letter

UNIVERSITY OF
SCHOOL OF MEDICINE

December 20, 1988

Mr. Russell Kleiser, Dealer Support Manager
NISSAN MOTOR CORP. USA
P.O. Box 191
Gardena, CA 90247-7638

Dear Russ:

The Grand Prix Gala has become recognized as one of the premiere international events of the Miami social season. The Gala, attended by approximately 1,000 people, kicks off the Grand Prix race weekend, and raises substantial funds for many worthwhile charitable causes. This year's Gala will be held on Friday, March 3, 1989 at the Omni International Hotel, and will raise funds for the U/Miami Burn Center, The Mailman Center for Child Development and The Learning Experience School.

We would like to invite Nissan Corporation to join with us as a major sponsor to underwrite a dining gallery area at the cocktail reception of the Gala. We anticipate the Gala to have three major areas featuring various international food including Oriental, European and Miami Beach style buffets.

We would like to suggest that the Nissan dining gallery reflect a visit to the Orient. The high dining drama begins with a garden of delights from Japan, and points East, including an extraordinary presentation of Sushi and Sashimi, joining an additional array of Japanese dishes prepared to order and served by oriental chefs. Our party design staff will set up an appropriate Oriental setting which would include individuals in appropriate traditional Japanese costumes.

The cost of sponsoring this dining gallery, for food and decor, would be Ten Thousand Dollars ($10,000.00). We certainly would be happy to recognize Nissan support by appropriate signage at the dining gallery, as well as recognition in all print material for the event and extensive individual coverage by international press.

Following the two-hour cocktail reception, there will be a spectacular stage show in the Main Ballroom, featuring ROBERTA FLACK IN CONCERT.

The underwriting of the major cocktail areas would certainly help us to maximize our fundraising efforts. We would be delighted to answer any questions or concerns you may have. We look forward to your early response.

Sincerely,

Ralph & Lourdes Sanchez
Executive Chairpersons

Office of Development for Medical Affairs
P.O. Box 016960 (R100)
Miami, Florida 33101
(305) 547-6256

television commercials. A major source of underwriting funds is corporate advertising and marketing budgets. Fast-food chains, supermarkets, airlines, car rental companies, and department stores can be excellent sources for underwriting portions or entire events in return for having their name prominently listed on all printed materials and in the news media in connection with the event. It's just another form of advertising for these companies and can be a better way to reach certain markets while also being good citizens (see chapter 3).

Companies can also play a major role in helping to raise money through participation in ad books, cooperative ads in newspaper, radio and TV, and what are known as point-of-purchase sales. In this case, the company agrees to donate a certain amount of money for each product purchased during a specific time.

For the Muscular Dystrophy Association (MDA), the Gillette Company donates a certain amount of money for every Gillette product purchased during September. Figure 2-8 shows a sweep-stakes entry sponsored by CITGO and American Airlines, also to benefit MDA, and a cents-off coupon from Procter & Gamble to benefit Special Olympics.

Sometimes companies will donate items for charities to raffle or auction off, such as airline tickets, fast-food coupons, jewelry, or trips. This is a great revenue booster. These sources are important because they often are 100 percent profit. When the University of Miami Burn Center held a beach party, the local Budweiser distrib-utor supplied beer at cost—$400. The center made $7,000 that day selling the beer at $2 a mug.

Checking It Twice

To double-check that you have anticipated all your costs, take your completed budget sheet and mentally walk through the event: Where will it be held? Do you need to pay for parking? Valet or security? What will the entrance look like? Do you need props? Balloons? Mimes? Klieg lights? Where will registration be held? How many tables and chairs will you need for registration? How many people do you need to handle it? Are they volunteers or paid

Figure 2-8. Sample Point-of-Purchase Sales Devices

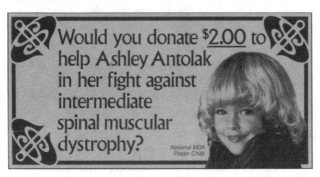

staff? Where are the staging areas? What equipment will be needed there? Continue visualizing each area of the event, what's needed for it, and what it will cost.

Ways to Boost Income

Besides the price you charge for the event itself, there are a number of ways to enhance the amount you raise. Among them are:

Advertising

Just as at big sporting events, you can sell advertising at your event. Sell space on your walls, doors, and tables. Sponsors might purchase any one or all three. At the tables, the company's name might be displayed on a bouquet of balloons or on the table assignment cards people receive at registration.

Balloons

While customarily used at auctions, these can also complement other types of events. Have people walk around offering helium-filled balloons for sale. Each balloon contains a number that corresponds to one of a number of gifts, which you had the foresight to get donated and which are displayed prominently. Set balloon prices at about a quarter of the cost of the prizes they redeem (if the prize is a dinner for two worth $40, balloons should sell for about $10). Because the value of what's in the balloons is guaranteed to be more than what they pay, guests have a greater incentive to purchase the balloons. Among the items you might want to solicit are facials, manicures, rounds of golf, and dinners for two.

Duck Pond/Grab Bag

This game is just what it sounds like. Get a kiddie pool, fill it with water, and set a bunch of plastic ducks loose to bob about. Before placing them in the water, mark numbers on their bellies with a waterproof pen. People then buy a duck and get the prize bearing the same number as the one on the duck. You can alter this by matching the "pond" to your event. At a Hawaiian luau, pick plastic pineapples out of a volcano. At a University of Miami Burn Center event we used stuffed dalmations (the group's symbol) with numbers wrapped around their necks. Besides the prize, buyers got to take home their stuffed dogs. In this game, everyone wins something.

Guess the Number of . . .

Get a big container and fill it with jellybeans, marbles, coins, etc. Or fill a treasure chest with money and let people guess how much it contains. Or get a huge vegetable and have people guess how much it weighs (no, they cannot pick it up). You, of course, need to know the answer ahead of time. At the end of the day, reveal the answer and pick a winner from all those entries with the correct answer or split the winnings among them. This is a good addition to festivals and various outdoor events.

Key Club

Sell keys, the corresponding locks to which are on the prizes. You can sell keys for donated bicycles, cars, boats, jet skis, motorcycles, or even items that don't normally have locks. In this game, not everyone will win.

Mini-Auction

Hold a brief auction at the ball or dinner. Get five or six big-ticket items (that have been donated, of course) and add in the table centerpieces. Keep it short. If this drags on too long, you'll ruin the flow of your dinner, dance, etc.

Program Book

Guests receive these booklets as they arrive. In them are a rundown of the program, a discussion of the organization and its goals, perhaps pictures from past events, a list of the committee members, perhaps a letter of support from a political bigwig, and as many ads as your committee could sell. Sell these the way you might for newspapers. Tell the potential advertisers how many people you plan to give the books to and something about the type of people who will attend. Sell ads of varying sizes—business-card-size (ten to a page), eighth-pages, quarter-, half-, and whole-page ads. For bigger-budget advertisers, sell them a whole page in platinum or silver and use that color for those pages.

For a sample ad rate chart and order form see figure 2-9.

If someone in the group has the capability of computerized desktop publishing, you can cut costs considerably. Try to get the printing underwritten to keep costs low, too. These books can be enormously profitable. For example, the Juvenile Diabetes Foundation at the University of Miami publishes one for its annual Love and Hope Ball. It resembles a school yearbook, thick with a hard cover, and nets the foundation $500,000 a year. Of course, the ball and its accompanying book have been an annual event for several years and have built a constituency. Also, the program book committee works year-round, starting the next book as soon as the ball is over. For examples of program books see figure 2-10.

Raffle/Door Prize

One way to get people involved who cannot attend your event is to sell them raffle tickets for prizes to be given away there. Maybe they won't buy a $250 ticket to a ball, but they might be willing to spend $10 or $20 on a chance to win something like a cruise. To encourage nonattendees to buy the raffle tickets, you must specify

Figure 2-9. Sample Ad Rates/Order Form

30th ANNIVERSARY
NATIONAL PARKINSON FOUNDATION
"GALA FOR HOPE"
ANNIVERSARY JOURNAL BOOK CONTRACT
FEBRUARY 28, 1988

I hereby authorize NPF to insert the enclosed advertisement in the 1988 **"Gala for Hope"** Souvenir Journal for the size indicated below. The Journal Size is 8½ x 11.

ADVERTISING RATES & SIZES:

		Copy Size	Bleed Size	Rate
_____	Back Cover	7½ x 10	8¾ x 11¼	$2,000.00
_____	Inside Cover	7½ x 10	8¾ x 11¼	$1,500.00
_____	Gold Pages	7½ x 10	8¾ x 11¼	$1,000.00
_____	Silver Pages	7½ x 10	8¾ x 11¼	$ 750.00
_____	Full Page B & W	7½ x 10	8¾ x 11¼	$ 500.00
_____	Half Page B & W Vertical	3¾ x 10	N/A	$ 275.00
_____	Half Page B & W Horinzontal	5 x 7½	N/A	$ 275.00
_____	Quarter Page B & W	3½ x 5	N/A	$ 175.00

_____ I prefer to make a contribution of $ _____ ($25.00) minimum

_____ Have my name listed in the Thank You Page.

_____ Do not list my name in the Thank You Page.

Check enclosed for $ _____

Special positions sold on
first come basis.
(Advertiser Please Print)

Make check payable to:
NATIONAL PARKINSON FOUNDATION
1501 N.W. 9th Avenue, Bob Hope Road
Miami, Florida 33136

COMPANY: _____

NAME: _____ PHONE: _____

ADDRESS: _____

CITY: _____ STATE: _____ ZIP: _____

AUTHORIZED SIGNATURE: _____ DATE: _____

TYPE AND PLACEMENT OF AD: _____

☐ Please repeat our previous ad.
☐ Ad enclosed.
☐ Please have a representative call us.

Please retain yellow copy for your files. For further information and/or assistance, please call Raquel Lazo (305) 547-6666 out of State (800) 327-4545. The above ad is tax deductible, as provided by law, either as a business advertising expense or as a charitable contribution. Your support of the National Parkinson Foundation is sincerely appreciated and will be used to assist us in our continuous endevor to seek the cause and cure of the Parkinson Syndrome, and other allied neurological disorders. (i.e. Alzheimer's, Stroke, Spinal Cord Injuries, etc.)

SOLD BY: _____

- -

FOR INTERNAL USE ONLY:

Date ad copy received _____ Record Number _____

Date approved: _____

Date sent to printer: _____ Ad Number _____

Figure 2-10. Sample Program Books

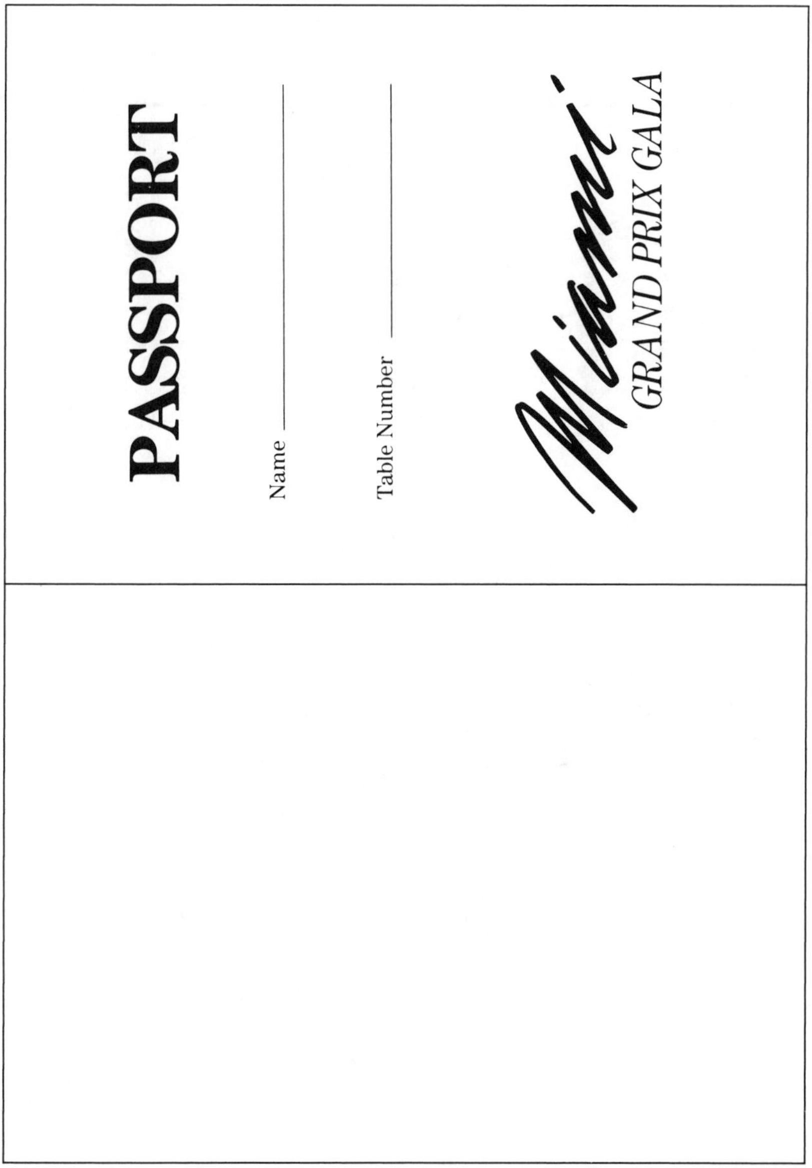

Honorary Chairpersons
Tony and Joyce Burns

Chairperson
Eleanor Kosow

Co-Chairpersons
Kathy Simkins
Blanca Suarez
Rosario Vadia

Corporate Sponsors
BELLSOUTH MOBILITY
MARTINI & ROSSI
NISSAN MOTOR CORPORATION

Special Thanks
Continental Companies
The Rose Club
Johnnie Walker
Eastern Airlines
Tanqueray Gin
Cordials by Maria Brizard
Hennessy Cognac V.S.O.P.
Morgan Music Company
Milton B. Suchin

Dear Friends,

It is with great pleasure that we welcome you to the 1989 Grand Prix Gala to benefit the UM/JM Burn Center, Mailman Child Development Center and The Learning Experience School. Your continued support of these worthwhile causes is deserving of a wonderful evening.

Ladies and gentlemen, start your engines and join us for an evening of international dining and entertainment by one of the greatest singers of our time, Roberta Flack.

The 1989 Grand Prix Gala is an excellent beginning of a weekend filled with exciting festivities, sun, fun and an opportunity to show off our community in its best light.

We would like to thank all those who worked so unselfishly to make this evening a success.

Enjoy yourselves and thank you again for your encouragement and support.

Sincerely,

Lourdes & Ralph

Lourdes and Ralph Sanchez
Executive Chairpersons

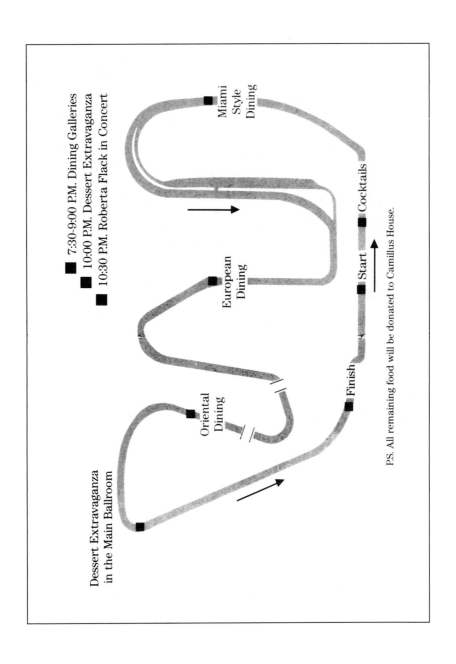

Dessert Extravaganza
in the Main Ballroom

Oriental
Dining

European
Dining

Miami
Style
Dining

Start

Cocktails

Finish

7:30-9:00 P.M. Dining Galleries

10:00 P.M. Dessert Extravaganza

10:30 P.M. Roberta Flack in Concert

P.S. All remaining food will be donated to Camillus House.

Honorary Committee

Mrs. Bernard Abel
Ms. Norma Jean Abraham
Mr. and Mrs. Emilio Alonso-Mendoza
Mrs. Ivette Arango
Mr. Raul Arango
Mr. and Mrs. Ricardo Arregui
Mr. and Mrs. Stephen N. Ashman
Mrs. Ruby Bacardi
Mr. and Mrs. Jose Manuel Baeza
Mr. and Mrs. Wendell Beard
Mr. and Mrs. Joaquin Blaya
Dr. and Mrs. Irwin Boruchow
Mrs. Nora Bulnes
Mr. and Mrs. Alvaro M. Cabrera
Mr. and Mrs. Fernando Capablanca
Mr. and Mrs. Randy Coleman
Mr. Walter Crosson
Mr. and Mrs. Luis Del Pozo
Mr. and Mrs. Alan Dubson
Mr. and Mrs. George Feldenkreis
Mr. and Mrs. Emerson Fittipaldi
Mr. and Mrs. Jose Freixas
Mr. and Mrs. Diego Gasso
Dr. and Mrs. Jeffrey Hammond
Mr. and Mrs. Abel Holtz
Mr. Daniel Holtz
Mr. and Mrs. F. Glenn Jackman
Ms. Karin Kerwin

Steering Committee

Marta Arboleya
Dorothy Ash
Carole Christoff
Harriet Dash
Remedios Diaz-Oliver
Harry Freedman
Dr. Jeffrey Hammond
Monica Heftler
Yolanda T. Hospital
Kelley Kosow-Werner
Martha Mishcon
Georgina Montoulieu
Maria Rosa Lopez Munoz
Joann Ryburn
Ana Soler
Maria Vadia
Dr. C. Gillon Ward
Ruth A. Wiesenthal-Gold
Connie Willman

Honorary Committee

Mr. and Mrs. Russell Kleiser
Mr. Ralph Lawson
Ms. Marcy Lefton
Mr. and Mrs. Robert W. Leider
Mr. and Mrs. German Leiva
Dr. Aida T. Levitan
Mr. and Mrs. Juan Lopez
Mr. and Mrs. Robert Marlin
Mr. and Mrs. Fausto Marquez
Mr. Ron Mashburn
Mr. Thomas D. Mignanelli
Mr. and Mrs. Carlos Migoya
Mr. and Mrs. Leonard Miller
Mr. and Mrs. Benjamin Nameth
Mr. Steven Neckman
Dr. and Mrs. Ferdie Pacheco
Mr. Robert Pascal
Mr. Carlos Plana
Dr. and Mrs. Willie Robinson
Mr. Fausto Sanchez
Mr. and Mrs. Eduardo Sardiña
Mr. and Mrs. Rob Schechter
Mr. Lee Brian Schrager
Mr. Byron L. Sparber
Mr. Jose Valdes-Fauli
Dr. and Mrs. C. Gillon Ward
Mr. and Mrs. Sherwood Weiser

FASHIONATION '86

Last year Americans spent $220 million a day on illicit drugs. Dealers are peddling drugs on almost every block, in every city. They're pushing to high school and college students throughout the country.

Informed Families is a volunteer organization whose major goal is to combat drug abuse among youth. The University of Miami's Spanish Family Guidance Center has been developing scientific strategies for the treatment of behavioral problems associated with drug abuse.

Fashionation '86 is the first collaborative effort between these two organizations. Together, we can work toward a solution to this urgent problem. Thank you for joining us this evening and giving us your support. We appreciate it. But more importantly, so will our children.

Special thanks
to
Bloomingdale's at The Falls
for their gracious contribution.
And to
McFarland & Drier Advertising
and
Parties by Neil
for their exceptional creative services
and fine professionalism.

In appreciation to

The Falls

and The Courtelis Company
for their outstanding generosity and support.

Patrons

Barnett Bank of South Florida
Bloomingdale's at The Falls
Knight-Ridder Newspapers, Inc.
Southeast Bank, N.A.
Mr. & Mrs. Charles Wilson
Xerox Corporation

Sponsors

Mr. & Mrs. Ted Arison
Burger King Corporation
Mr. & Mrs. Patrick Cesarano
Dr. Raquel Cohen
The Continental Companies
Mr. & Mrs. Alec P. Courtelis
Mr. & Mrs. Joel Eaton
Dr. & Mrs. Bernard Fogel
Mrs. Olivia Hallet
Mr. & Mrs. Frederick Havenick
Hialeah Hospital
Dr. & Mrs. Ronald Hinds
Mr. & Mrs. John R. Hoehl

Mr. & Mrs. H. Kassner
Mr. & Mrs. Thomas Krause
Mr. & Mrs. Terrence L. McKinley
Mr. & Mrs. Gerald F. Richman
Mr. & Mrs. Sheldon Rosenthal
Smathers and Thompson
Southern Bell
Drs. Jay Vandenbosch
  & Ana Rivas Vasquez
Drs. Manuel & Maria Viamonte
WPLG/TV 10
Mr. & Mrs. David Weaver
Mr. & Mrs. Dean Willman

F A S H I O N A T I O N '86

Hotel Inter-Continental Miami
December 12, 1986

7:00 .... Cocktails and Silent Auction
Entertainment by The Greater Miami Opera

8:30 .... Dinner
Entertainment by Sylvia Bennett

9:15 .... Recognition and Appreciation
Fashion Show, Shops of The Falls

9:45 .... Live Auction
Joel Langbaum, Auctioneer

10:15 .... Performance by Billy Hufsey

10:30 .... Special Guest Star, Phyllis Diller

Major Auction Benefactors

Ariel Human Performance Center
Bolae
Carnival Cruise Lines
Kings Bay Country Club
Mayor's Jewelers
"Miami Vice," Universal City Studios, NBC
Ned Moulton
Safety Harbor Spa
Scat Hovercraft

Special Donors

Audrey Rubin Designs
Battaglia at The Falls
Blackwell Walker Fascell & Hoehl
Bliss & Nvitray, Inc.
Bloomingdale's at The Falls
Cellular One
Eastern Airlines
Ecuatoriana de Aviacion
Dr. & Mrs. J. Evans
Exotic Boat Rentals
Fisher Island

Floyd Pearson Richman Greer Weil Zack & Brumbaugh, P.A.
The Greater Miami Opera
Harris Travel
Interval International
Lily's at The Falls
Miami Workout
Raleigh Ltd.
Tropical Balloon Rides
Williams Island

Fashionation '86 Chairman:

Cheri Rosenthal

Steering Committee

Gerry Bowenkamp
Pan Courtelis
Harry Freedman
Miriam Hinds
Susannah McLean
Ana Padilla
Peggy Sapp
José Szapocznik, Ph.D.

Organizing Committee Chairmen

Sue Cesarano
Sue Fast
Norma Hanna, Ph.D.
Susannah McLean
Ana Padilla
Betty Park
Gwen Richman
Connie Willman

Organizing Committee

Joan Andros
Gerry Bowenkamp
Mary Eaton
Joan Ewald
Marilyn Greenfield
Olivia Hallet
Florence Hecht
Mary Frances Irvin
Mary-Jo Jasinski
Robin Joseph
Roslyn Joseph
Teddy Kassner
Martha Kazanzas
Randall Kettle
Shelley Krause
Janice Lacapra
Kathy Lary
Barbara Lipcon
Zammy Migdal
Mary Riley
Cheri Rosenthal
Terry Schechter
Dorothy Schlissel
Mark Singer
Rhoni Tannenbaum
Debbie Vieta

Thank you to the following staff members for their hard work and dedicated efforts.

University of Miami
Barbara Bushnell
Esteban Garcia
Sylvia Kaminsky
Teresita Lanza
Ana Padilla
Maria Padron

Informed Families
Ana Perez-Vidal, Psy. D.
Rita Friedman
Robert Johnson
Beverly Longuil
Peggy Sapp
Shara Schild

In appreciation for services rendered by:

Crooks Printing
The Main Event
J. Mendez Photography
Runways
Jay Sugarman and Joel Langbaum of
Jay Sugarman Auctioneers

Paid Professional Services:
Harry Freedman and Associates, Inc.
Laser Productions
Michael Designs
Philly Sound Machine
Production Dynamics

Fashion Show Participants

Alessandro
Ann Taylor
Banana Republic
Caché
Casablanca
Clappers
Coverage
Exit Shops
Farouche
Kiki at The Falls
Laura Ashley

Limited Express
New Man at Bip
Norka
Oxygene Paris
Peck & Peck
Polo/Ralph Lauren Shop
Private Collection
Raphael
Renegade
Sara Fredericks
T. Edwards

Many thanks to Bloomingdale's
Beauty Concepts at The Falls
for hair and make-up design.

The Falls

that the winner need not be present. You can also sell additional tickets during the event. Display the prizes (sports equipment, cases of wine or beer, posters of a cruise or airline trip). You can also hold a 50–50 raffle: people win half the money collected, the charity keeps the other half (these are especially popular at festivals and other large events). At banquets, you can raffle off the centerpieces, or award them to those who buy the most raffle tickets at each table.

CHECKLIST

☐ How much cash does your group have available?

☐ How much can it lay out before money starts coming in?

☐ Is the proposed event within your price range?

☐ Should you consider joining forces with other groups?

☐ Calculate budget using the worksheet in figure 2-1.

☐ Look for corporate underwriters.

☐ Set ticket prices.

☐ Double-check the budget by mentally walking through each step to make sure you have allowed for all expenses.

☐ Consider what types of income-boosters might work at your event.

Chapter 3

The Big Picture

Successful events depend on the coordination of hundreds of large and small tasks, all of which must get done correctly and on time. The best formula for making sure this happens is to have one competent person in charge who then marshals sufficient workers to attend to everything. This person, called the event manager, oversees the event from start to finish. The event manager's main task is to form committees and assign responsibilities, keeping a close eye on the money and the calendar (see the special event countdown at the end of this chapter).

The person chosen for this job should have some previous experience supervising events. It can be the organization's executive director, if this person has the time to devote to it—count on 50 percent or more of his or her working time for at least the three months leading to the event. If your organization is big enough to have a fund-raising director, he or she would normally serve in this capacity. If you don't have either, consider hiring someone from the community on a short-term basis, if you can afford it.

Sometimes, there is an economical alternative—a competent, experienced volunteer, many of whom have more experience than the professionals. Some people produce events as volunteers on a regular basis and grow quite adept at it. To find someone like this, ask around and check social pages in the newspapers to see who is active in other organizations.

When *Ms.* magazine planned its tenth anniversary party in the early 1980s, it was to be a two-city event, traveling from New York City to Philadelphia and back. The aim was to pay tribute to women working together and to showcase the magazine and its founder, Gloria Steinem. The "Today" show was to follow Steinem as she traveled from New York to Philadelphia by train, attended a luncheon, then returned to New York.

From the outset, it was clear that such a complex event needed one strong manager to coordinate it. It was also evident that there were a lot of aspirants to the job, including some from the magazine's staff, the "Today" show, and the various women's groups involved. When it came down to who had the time to handle the top job properly, one woman emerged. She was a volunteer from Women's Way—the Philadelphia umbrella organization of women's groups sponsoring the luncheon—who had organized women's rallies. She oversaw Steinem's train trip from New York to Philadelphia, the luncheon at Philadelphia's elegant Bellevue Stratford Hotel, the train ride back to New York, the party *Ms.* magazine held there, and the "Today" show's coverage of the day's events. Had all those who wanted to be in charge proceeded on their own, the result would have been chaos and disaster. With one organized person at the helm, the event came off without a hitch.

Picking an Event Coordinator

If you will be selecting a coordinator from outside your organization (or are considering naming a group member who has not served your organization in that capacity before), there are some questions you should ask first. Among them:

- How many events have you supervised before?
- What were they?
- Were they for publicity or fund raising?
- If they were for publicity, how many people attended?

- If they were fund raisers, how much money did they raise?
- Did they follow a budget?
- How much time do you have to devote to an event?
- Would you work out of your home or the organization's office?
- What kinds of people skills do you have?
- How do you function under pressure?
- Do you have any references or news clippings in connection with previous events?

Once you get references, check them out. Ask questions. If you are considering a volunteer, you'll need to go about this more delicately than if you are planning to hire someone. Nevertheless, it is vital that the potential manager's abilities be fully assessed before he or she gets the job.

The Event Coordinator's Job

The primary functions of the event manager are fund raising, promotion, recruitment of volunteers, and management. Consider getting cochairmen so they can divide the work. This is also helpful because if one is unable to complete his or her task, there will still be someone in charge.

Even the most promising event can fail if the wrong person is put in charge, as happened in Florida. In an effort to get new community residents involved in a university, the school's board courted newcomers of a nearby neighborhood in which homes were valued at more than $1 million. Luncheons were held to familiarize these affluent people with the various programs and needs of the university. They were then asked to help in whatever way they could.

Among the potential new volunteers to emerge from this group was a very enthusiastic woman. She volunteered to chair a major fund-raising effort. Because she was new to the area, no one knew whether she was qualified, but she seemed readily available, motivated, and creative. She offered to host a fund-raising party at her home to bring in other influential people.

When she said, "Don't worry, I'll handle everything," that should have alerted the group to trouble. Over the course of the next several months, she kept assuring the group that everything was in great shape. But, in the end, fewer than a dozen people attended a party that was supposed to have 50 to 100 in attendance. The group lost $500 in expenses on an event that was to have brought in $20,000, along with dozens of new long-range supporters.

The organization made two mistakes in this case:

1. No one checked on the woman's experience elsewhere.

2. No one from the staff was sufficiently involved. A cochairman should have been appointed, someone established in the group and the community, to make sure all necessary tasks were attended to.

Getting Started

One you have someone in place, the person's first job is to get everyone together to break the event into components, determine what tasks need doing, and assign people to various committees.

TIP: Get everything in writing. Assume nothing.

To keep things organized, get a loose-leaf notebook with dividers, which should be titled:

- Time line and assignments.
- Budget.
- Committees.
- Correspondence.
- Entertainment.
- Invitations and printing.
- Accommodations.
- Travel.
- Program book.
- Photography.

- Registration.
- Schedule script.
- Welcome kit.

Add whatever tabs are appropriate for your event. The front page of each section has a checklist of what needs to be done to complete each task. Behind that go copies of correspondence, bids, contracts, agreement letters, etc. The notebook should be kept in the office or the home of the primary volunteer for easy reference.

TIP: Don't take anything out of the book. Make copies if you need anything from it.

The advantage to this system is that everything pertaining to the event is in one easily accessible space, it's a handy reference for the event chairman to bring to meetings, and it will be an invaluable resource the next time the group plans an event. After awhile you'll have a library of reference materials. It also will help the next set of chairmen when they set out to do their first event or when another group needs help with one.

When the National Adoption Center decided to have a benefit tied to the opening of the Ringling Brothers-Barnum & Bailey Circus in New York City, an official asked me to manage it. I could not arrange to be out of Florida for the necessary length of time and did not think the job could be done properly long distance. But because I'd run a similar event before, I offered the group my loose-leaf notebook. All the event manager had to do was go through it and copy the format. By using the book, the charity's chairman knew what needed to be done, the right questions to ask, and whether the special events firm the group hired was doing its job.

The notebook is another reason why you should get everything in writing. When you order something, get a purchase order. If you sign a contract, get a copy. When someone agrees to donate something, send that person a confirmation letter specifying the exact date you expect to receive the item or money. Put copies of everything in the book.

TIP: Have a separate page with a list of all your key people, their home and work phones, FAX numbers, and addresses. Do the same sort of list of your major vendors.

Staying on Track

It's important to create a time line listing everything that needs to be done. Set it up as shown below and put it in the front of the notebook.

DATE (to be completed)	TASK	PERSON

Assign staff and volunteers to each task, and send each worker written confirmation of his or her specific assignments. For reinforcement, if you have an office, put up a big poster or sheet of paper that lists the tasks of each committee, then check the items off as they are completed. While you are getting organized, establish the pecking order. Make it clear who will have the final word. This might be the event coordinator, a knowledgeable chairman, or the group's executive director.

It's especially important to designate a leader in groups with many powerful or influential people. In some cases, you may wind up with the honorary chairman, executive director, chief surgeon, and town mayor—all of whom are accustomed to being in charge—wanting to take command. Just because they are in charge elsewhere does not mean they should be in charge of the event.

Financial Control

Get bids for everything. The costs of sound, lights, and food can vary by thousands of dollars. Make sure bids are for comparable products and services. If you are dealing with services such as food or lighting, get recommendations from friends and associates, then obtain at least three bids. Pick the bid you like best, then try to negotiate for a lower price.

TIP: It may be easier to get a lower price if you are planning more than one event a year or could tie it in with other events.

In 1987 the Miami Design Preservation League wanted to do a spectacular outdoor concert with a big band, such as Cab Calloway, for Art Deco Weekend. Another charity, the Children's Home Society (a shelter for abused children), also wanted to do something different from the traditional black-tie, sit-down dinner it usually hosted. The groups decided to work together to bring in Calloway and his band. The event manager had previously worked with a booking agent in New York City who handled many of the old-time big bands. He was told the two charities wanted to bring Cab Calloway to town, sharing whatever expenses were not underwritten. The agent said Calloway was a big horse-racing fan, so the entertainment committee chairman contacted a Hialeah Racetrack official and asked if the track would like to help sponsor Calloway's appearance in Miami. He asked for a written proposal, which was sent, suggesting that the racetrack pay for some of the expenses in exchange for hosting a Cab Calloway Day at the track. The track official agreed.

Calloway went to the track, which covered some of his travel costs and made a donation to the charities. A race was named after him and he was introduced between races. Calloway and his band performed an outdoor benefit concert Sunday for Art Deco Weekend. The preceding night, they entertained at the Children's Home Society ball. (During an auction at the ball, an autographed Calloway record and baton sold for $10,000.)

Calloway lost a bit of money betting at the track. The track officials were pleased with the free publicity they got as a result of his appearance. Both organizations made money, sharing the costs of the few expenses not covered by sponsors.

Finding Underwriting

To get underwriting—otherwise known as cash—from companies or individuals, you have to give something away. Usually, charities offer recognition in exchange for goods or services. Underwriting is any contribution of money, items, or in-kind services from individuals, businesses, and corporations, that helps offset the outlay of cash by a nonprofit organization. The company donates the items or cash to underwrite major costs, such as food, sound, lights, or printing. The charity reciprocates by including the company's name in advertising, on the invitations, on banners at the event, or in any other agreed-upon manner. The fewer things it has to pay cash for, the more money the charity can put toward its cause.

Art Deco Weekend on Miami Beach is an excellent example of getting maximum fund raising with major underwriting. The annual weekend-long event helps the Miami Design Preservation League raise money for its numerous historic preservation projects. Normally, a host of sponsors is lined up, including at least one airline, a beer company, and a hotel. The airline flies in VIPs and celebrities who will entertain at the show; the sponsoring hotel furnishes them with rooms. The beer sponsor pays the league about $20,000 for the exclusive right to sell beer at the well-attended event. That money is used to help pay for cleanup, posters, sound, and lights. The league also sells booths to exhibitors, who then sell their wares there. This money pays for the tents and booths, with some left over. In addition, the league operates a booth selling art deco posters, T-shirts, and gifts, which adds to the profit. A $100-per-person ball kicks off the weekend and features the same artists who will appear throughout the event.

Another possibility is to find an angel—an individual who has the means and desire to support your cause.

In 1987, when raising money for AIDS research and treatment was still not widely acceptable, the University of Miami's Clinical AIDS Research Program wanted to ask Elizabeth Taylor to participate in its function. Taylor is an outspoken champion of AIDS research and treatment and was chairman of the American Foundation for AIDS Research. The Miami group learned that it would have to guarantee to raise $1 million in order for Taylor to attend. The group needed someone to underwrite the event to ensure this.

I had worked with Celia Lipton Farris, a well-known Palm Beach philanthropist and star of the British stage, on several charitable fund raisers and so approached her about this one. She initially agreed to donate the difference between what the charity raised and the $1 million, then decided to donate $1.2 million and hosted a lavish party at her home as the kickoff to the 1988 "Extraordinary Evening with Elizabeth Taylor." In all, the event raised $2.2 million.

Conflicts of Interest

At times there may be conflicts between a charity's goals or beliefs and those of the corporations that want to underwrite an event. Some conflicts are obvious, such as a tobacco company sponsoring a lung association or cancer society event. Such situations pose potential problems to which charities must be ever alert. Although the corporation's intentions may be sincere, if potential donors find the connection offensive, the company's participation may harm your fund raising rather than enhance it.

Such a potential problem arose in the planning of a golf tournament benefit for the Addictions Institute, a Miami center that trains counselors to work with people with addiction-related problems. The event was sponsored by the Miami Beach Chamber of Commerce. The area Budweiser distributor wanted to be a sponsor, but charity organizers demurred. They realized it would be in bad taste to allow Budweiser to be the major sponsor of an event that benefits people who cannot handle drugs, including alcohol. When the charity's staff discussed the problem with Budweiser officials, the beer distributor suggested the charity approach Hooters, a popular area beer and chicken wings chain. The restaurant agreed to be a major sponsor and the event became the Hooters Superweek Golf Tournament. The restaurant donated money, food, and advertising and hosted several preview events. The Budweiser distributor served as a minor sponsor, donating beverages (beer, non-alcoholic beer, and soft drinks), which were provided along with dinner to the golfers. In exchange for its donation, Budweiser's name appeared on the back of golf carts and in the program while Hooters was more prominently featured in banners and promotional material for the event.

If such matters are handled with sensitivity, it's possible to avoid offending either your potential donors or the companies that you may want to approach for underwriting or sponsorship in the future.

Seeking Support

There are a number of ways to solicit underwriting. One is to have an underwriting party. Draw up a list of the items you would like to have underwritten. Prior to the party, contact as many businesses as you can and ask each one to sponsor something. Then invite everyone to an underwriting party, usually a cocktail party with light refreshments, often at someone's home. At the party, announce the commitments you've already received and thank those companies for their participation. That should spur some of the others who have not yet committed. That's when you distribute the list of items that still needed underwriting.

Some groups leave the underwriting chores to the events manager or someone he or she designates; others use a committee to contact potential sponsors for support. Usually, the more people on the committee, the more underwriting you'll get.

TIP: Be prepared to spell out exactly what you will give the underwriting company in exchange for its support—i.e., tickets to the event, banners posted prominently, advertising, its name in the program book, etc. As with everything else, put it in writing.

Another way to get underwriting is to first go after a radio station or newspaper as a sponsor. Generally, such organizations will agree to give you a certain amount of advertising time/space to promote your event. Once you have that, it's easier to line up other sponsoring businesses interested in getting some exposure for supporting a worthwhile cause.

When looking for a radio station's support, seek out a station whose listeners are the people you want to attract to your event. All radio stations can tell you precisely who their listeners are—

Figure 3-1. Sample List of Items for Underwriting

```
ITEM(S)              ITEMS FOR UNDERWRITING   ESTIMATED AMOUNT
                        PARTIAL LISTING
1.   Advertising...  ...  ...  ...  ...  ...$_____

2.   Awards...  ...  ...  ...  ...  ...  ...$_____

3.   Dinner
         Food & Service  ...  ...  ...  ...$_____

         Liquor...  ...  ...  ...  ...  ...$_____

4.   Flowers & Decor ...  ...  ...  ...  ...$_____

5.   Favors...  ...  ...  ...  ...  ...  ...$_____

6.   Music
         Cocktail Party  ...  ...  ...  ...$_____

         Dinner & Show  ...  ...  ...  ...$_____

7.   Printing
         Invitations...  ...  ...  ...  ...$_____

         Tickets..  ...  ...  ...  ...  ...$_____

         Press Packets.  ...  ...  ...  ...$_____

         Program Book..  ...  ...  ...  ...$_____

         Signage..  ...  ...  ...  ...  ...$_____

8.   Regular Cocktail Party
         Food & Liquor  ...  ...  ...  ...$_____

         Service..  ...  ...  ...  ...  ...$_____

9.   Photographers (2)..  ...  ...  ...  ...$_____

10.  Sound & Light Equipment.  ...  ...  ...$_____

11.  Underwriting Party
         Food & Liquor.  ...  ...  ...  ...$_____

         Service..  ...  ...  ...  ...  ...$_____

12.  Transportation for Celebrities
         Air Fare.  ...  ...  ...  ...  ...$_____

         Limousines ...  ...  ...  ...  ...$_____
```

their ages, median income, and listening habits. This is the information they use to sell commercials. Ask who their listeners are.

In seeking a radio station to sponsor a benefit show by artist Peter Max, the event manager looked for an oldies station that attracted people in their 30s and 40s, people who would recognize and identify with his art. When seeking a station to promote a chili festival, the event manager went to a country-western station that attracted a wider age group and more working-class families, who were most likely to attend the event.

If you or anyone in your group knows someone influential at a newspaper or a radio or television station, have that person contact the media person to let him or her know someone will soon be in touch about getting support for a charitable cause. This can help pave the way.

In Balance

It sounds almost too simple to mention, but make sure you collect all money due. Although the best way to handle this is to collect it up front, you cannot always do so (for example, when dealing with big corporations at which there are sometimes delays in cutting checks). Don't forget about it.

Try to collect all of the money from people attending the event before they get in the door. It's customary to require a check when people reserve a block of seats. If they don't send in a check, call and ask when you can expect it, or suggest they use a credit card.

Accepting credit cards will cost your group 1 to 6 percent, but because they are easy for people to use, they can boost sales. The percentage charged varies with the card and the sponsoring institution.

TIP: You can sometimes negotiate a lower percentage with bank-related cards (Visa and MasterCards offered by local banks).

At an auction, antique show or a-thon, where spur-of-the-moment purchasing is likely to occur, credit cards can sometimes double the amount you make. At a ball or dinner, they may not make much difference.

There is a downside to credit cards, too. They can be time-consuming because you often have to call to determine whether a person's credit is good. You'll need a telephone line to check credit. And it can be embarrassing for the donor if you find out his credit is not good. You will have to buy the machines you process the charge slips with and sometimes the slips themselves. If you are having a small-scale event, it's not worth your time (or the bank's) to open an account. But if you plan to have several events or one large one, it may pay off.

Whenever possible, collect the money before the day of the event. When that's not possible, make sure your registration committee is well briefed on who still has not paid and how to encourage guests to pay without alienating them. The committee might suggest the person pay by check or credit card at the door. A possible script might go like this: "We're trying to keep our costs as low as possible, so the greatest amount of money possible can go to the charity, Mr. Maxwell. It would be very helpful if we could have your payment tonight rather than billing you."

If all else fails, have the guest sign a slip indicating he or she agrees to pay. Bill these people promptly after the event.

Money Manager

One person should oversee accounting, maintaining the budget, banking, purchasing, ticket sales, legal matters, and collections. It's better if it's someone other than the event manager, who already has to take care of many details. If you have someone available and capable, it's good to have one person whose only responsibility is to handle the financial matters. One of the most important reasons to have a money manager is that many celebrities require payment by certified check on the night of the performance. Forget to bring it and the celebrity may forget the show he or she had planned.

TIP: Pin the check on your tux or dress—whatever you're wearing that night—several days in advance.

Keep a separate bank account for the event, if possible, so that these funds and expenses will not get mixed up with your regular funds and expenses.

If you accumulate large amounts of money ahead of time, put them in a money-market account to earn some interest. (Make sure you know how many checks you can write without incurring a lot of expense for doing so.)

Handling Ticket Sales

Tickets are the same as money and should be handled as such. The best way to maintain control of them is to number them in two spots—on the stub the group keeps and on the part the buyer keeps. Use these numbers for accounting.

If your members are selling your tickets, make sure everyone gets written instructions that state:

- How many tickets they are responsible to sell.
- The date by which they must be sold.
- That they remain responsible for those tickets even if they distribute them to others to sell.
- That money must be collected when they give people their tickets.

Also give each member a support packet that includes handouts explaining the event and the charity. Each member should develop a list of people he or she will approach. Encourage each member to write down a brief pitch that explains what the event is and why someone should buy the ticket. If there is a place to hang posters, give some to members to put up. The tickets themselves should include the name of the event, time, date, place, and cost per ticket. Each should also have a number.

TIP: To help prevent counterfeiting, include a special design, logo, or trademark on the ticket that would be hard to copy or select an unusual paper to have the tickets printed on.

Keep track of the tickets by number, matching the person who has them with a specific series of numbers. Boost sales by offering prizes to those who sell the most tickets. (Many businesses will donate dinners, haircuts, facials, makeup lessons, or rounds of golf. For bigger events, you might be able to offer a cruise or airline ticket.)

Give your sales force a list of contacts (chamber of commerce membership lists, Yellow Pages listings) and let your salespeople take the names of those they know personally. Divide up the rest among your salespeople so they can make cold calls. Make sure you include all the large companies in town as well as the stock brokerages, banks, law firms, and hospitals.

As an incentive, offer your sales forces free tickets if they are able to sell ten tickets to other people. (If you do this, be sure you've accounted for this in your expenses or can find a business willing to sponsor the cost of these tickets.)

For large, ticketed events, consider hiring a ticket service. Usually there's only one in the area—Ticketron and Ticketmaster are among the big ones. The telephone directory Yellow Pages will usually list them. For a percentage of sales (usually 1 to 3 percent), the company computerizes your tickets, sells them, and handles the bookkeeping and payment processing. At every outlet, they maintain a list of events for which they sell tickets, so you'll get added exposure there. And many will promote your event in their advertising. If you expect to sell 2,000 or more tickets, a ticket service is usually well worth the money.

Because the committee people will have the names of people who should be sent invitations, arrange to withhold tickets without a surcharge so they can be sold to the names your committee people have provided. If you give tickets to volunteers to sell, make sure you know which numbers have been assigned to each person. Make sure that anyone selling tickets knows when the unsold ones must be returned to you.

One thing that often happens unless you're careful is that you can get a false impression that you're sold out when you're not. It's important to keep track of how many tickets have actually been paid for.

Ticket-Accounting

Keep a ticket ledger, listing each ticket number and who has the ticket. On the night of the event, make sure you collect the ticket stubs to see how many people actually showed up and to enable you to reconcile the number with the amount of money you actually collected. You want to get all the unsold tickets back for the same reason.

TIP: Ticket sellers should get cash first, count it carefully, then deliver the ticket.

"Free" Tickets

Inevitably, some tickets get handed out to people who don't pay for them—the mayor, the news media, etc. Try to get these tickets underwritten. If that's not possible, try to get tickets back from anyone who is unable to use them so you can distribute them to VIPs, giving the donating business or individual credit.

Papering the House

If you want the place to look sold out even when it isn't, you can "paper the house"—give out tickets to civic organizations, police groups, retirement homes, etc. You can also do this if you've exhausted all avenues of selling tickets and feel you have made as much as you are going to. This is done only with theater or show events, not a sit-down meal. Do it only for events at which it doesn't cost you any more to fill up the seats. You can give the extra tickets to organizations that wouldn't normally attend, thereby exposing more people to your group.

CHECKLIST

☐ Key organization officials should examine the list of potential event managers, check references and experience, and then select the best one.

☐ The event manager forms committees, then drafts a list of tasks that need to be done, assigning each of them to a committee along with a date for completion.

☐ Start a loose-leaf notebook in which to document the event.

☐ Negotiate contracts with vendors, entertainers, etc.

☐ Seek underwriters.

☐ Keep an eye on the budget and/or appoint financial manager to handle bookkeeping and collections.

☐ Set up event bank account.

☐ Determine whether to allow use of credit cards for payment.

☐ Determine whether to use a ticket service or have staff and volunteers sell tickets.

SPECIAL EVENT COUNTDOWN

DATE   *TASK*   *PERSON*

6 TO 12 MONTHS AHEAD

_____   Decide event purpose (raise funds,   _____
             visibility, both)

_____   Choose theme   _____

_____   Visit possible sites   _____

_____   Research/approach chairmen   _____

_____   Research/appoint event manager   _____

_____   Form committees   _____

_____   Get cost estimates (site rental, food,   _____
             drinks, sound/lights, etc.)

_____   Get recommendations for music;   _____
             hold auditions

_____   Get bids for music   _____

_____   Get bids for decorations   _____

_____   Get bids for printing   _____

_____   Get bids for other major items   _____

_____   Draft initial budget   _____

_____   Designate someone to oversee   _____
             budget

_____   Research/approach honorees   _____

_____   Compile mailing list (individuals/   _____
             corporations)

_____   Check proposed date for potential   _____
             conflicts, finalize date in writing

_____   Get written contracts for catering,   _____
             entertainment, etc.

_____   Develop alternative site (if event is   _____
             outdoors)

_____   Consider pre-party event for   _____
            publicity or underwriting

_____   Invite/confirm VIPs   _____

_____   List items to get underwritten and   _____
            possible sources

_____   Order hold-the-date cards or other   _____
            event announcements

_____   Set marketing/public relations   _____
            schedule

_____   Develop press release and calendar   _____
            listings

_____   Select photographer; arrange for   _____
            photos of VIPs, chairmen, honorees

_____   Pick graphic artists; begin invitation   _____
            design

_____   Get biographical information on   _____
            VIPs, celebrities, honorees,
            chairmen

_____   Investigate need for special permits,   _____
            insurance, etc.

3 TO 6 MONTHS

_____   Begin monthly committee meetings   _____

_____   Write/send requests for funding or underwriting to major donors, corporations, sponsors   _____

_____   Review designs with graphic artist for invitations, programs, posters, etc.   _____

_____   Prepare final copy for invitations, return card, posters   _____

_____   Prepare final copy for tickets, parking permits, etc.   _____

_____   Order invitations, posters, tickets, etc.   _____

_____   Sign contract with band   _____

_____   Complete mailing lists for invitations and list of locations for posters   _____

_____   Finalize mailing lists; begin soliciting corporations and major donors   _____

_____   Obtain lists from honorees, VIPs   _____

_____   Obtain radio/TV sponsor, arrange public service announcements, promos   _____

_____   Set menu   _____

_____   Get written confirmation of celebrity participation/special needs   _____

_____   Finalize audio/visual contract   _____

_____   Select/order trophies/awards   _____

2 MONTHS AHEAD

_____   Hold underwriting or preview party   _____
            to coincide with mailing of
            invitations; invite media

_____   Assemble/address invitations (with   _____
            personal notes when possible)

_____   Mail invitations   _____

_____   Distribute posters   _____

_____   Finalize transportation and hotel   _____
            accommodations for VIPs,
            honorees

_____   Obtain contracts for decorations   _____
            and rental items

_____   Confirm TV/radio participation   _____

_____   Release press announcements about   _____
            celebrities, VIPs, honorees

_____   Follow up to confirm sponsorships   _____
            and underwriting

_____   Obtain logos from corporate   _____
            sponsors for printing

_____   Secure permits and insurance   _____

_____   Review needs for signs at   _____
            registration, elsewhere

_____   All major chairmen to review plans   _____

_____   Hold walk-through of event with   _____
            committee chairman at event site

_____   Review/revise budget, task sheets   _____

_____   Start phone follow-up solicitation   _____
            for sponsors of tables (corporate,
            VIP, committee)

1 MONTH AHEAD

_____ Phone follow-up to mailing list   _____
(ticket sales)

_____ Place newspaper ads   _____

_____ Follow up with news media for   _____
stories, on-air announcements

_____ Confirm staff for registration,   _____
hosting

_____ Write to VIPs, celebrities, program   _____
participants, confirming
participation

_____ Complete list of contents for VIP   _____
welcome packets

_____ Get enlarged site plan/room   _____
diagram

_____ Assign seats/tables   _____

_____ Give estimate of guests expected to   _____
caterer/food service

_____ Meet with all outside vendors,   _____
consultants to coordinate event

_____ Draft script   _____

2 WEEKS BEFORE

_____   Continue phone follow-ups for   _____
              ticket/table sales

_____   Continue assigning seats; set dais,   _____
              head table, speaker's platform

_____   Arrange to meet VIPs at airport,   _____
              train or hotel

_____   Confirm transportation schedules,   _____
              including airlines, trains, buses,
              cars/limos

_____   Confirm hotel accommodations   _____

_____   Prepare transportation and   _____
              accommodations (include flight
              number, airline, person assigned to
              meet flight)

_____   Confirm special security needed for   _____
              VIPs, event

_____   Prepare welcome packet for VIPs,   _____
              chairmen, and key staff

_____   Schedule deliveries of special   _____
              equipment, rentals

_____   Confirm set-up time with event site   _____

_____   Finalize plans with party decorator   _____

_____   Give caterer revised numbers   _____

_____   Meet with chairmen, key staff to   _____
              finalize any of the above

1 WEEK BEFORE

_____ Meet with all committees to ensure   _____
last-minute details are covered

_____ Finish phone follow-ups for sales   _____

_____ Confirm number attending   _____

_____ Finish seating/table arrangement   _____

_____ Hold training session with   _____
volunteers; finalize assignments

_____ Secure two or three volunteers to   _____
assist with emergencies

_____ Finalize registration staff/setup   _____

_____ Distribute seating chart, table   _____
assignments to hosts/hostesses

_____ Schedule pickup of any rented or   _____
loaned equipment

_____ Double-check delivery time with all   _____
vendors

_____ Reconfirm event site, hotel rooms,   _____
transportation

_____ Deliver final scripts to all committee   _____
chairmen, program participants

_____ Finalize catering guarantee   _____

_____ Finalize refreshments/meals for   _____
confirmed number of volunteers

_____ Make follow-up calls to news media   _____
for advance and event coverage

_____ Distribute additional fliers/posters   _____

_____ Hold final walk-through at site   _____

_____ Schedule rehearsals and volunteer   _____
assignments for day of event

_____ Establish amount of petty cash   _____
needed for tips and emergencies

_____ Pin cashier's check for celebrity,   _____
special permits, on outfit you will
wear to event

DAY BEFORE EVENT

_____   Lay out all clothes you will need day   _____
of event

_____   Make sure petty cash, checks are   _____
ready

EVENT DAY

_____	Arrive early (with all your clothes)	_____
_____	Unpack equipment, supplies and make sure nothing is missing	_____
_____	Be sure all VIPs are in place and have scripts	_____
_____	Reconfirm refreshment/meal schedule for volunteers	_____
_____	Check with volunteers to make sure all tasks covered	_____
_____	Set up registration area	_____
_____	Check sound/light equipment and staging before rehearsal	_____
_____	Hold rehearsal	_____
_____	Go over details with caterer	_____
_____	Make final calls/FAXes to media	_____

Chapter 4

All About Committees

QUESTION: What's a camel?
ANSWER: A horse created by a committee.

Okay, it's an old joke, but there's a reason it's been around a while: Committees left to their own devices can run amok. Every event needs to have a well-organized working committee, made up of motivated individuals who will make the event happen.

There have been many disastrous events that featured star-studded honorary committees. While these committees may have lent an air of sophistication and allure, they didn't sell tickets. Think of it in fishing terms: The honorary committee is the tasty bait; the working committee is the rod, reel, and hook. Organized properly, it's a winning combination.

Miami's Community Alliance Against AIDS used this combination successfully in 1988 when it sponsored "An Extraordinary Evening with Elizabeth Taylor." There were 20 honorary chairmen, each of whom committed to hosting a dinner at his or her home or a private club. Each chairman was assigned a celebrity who would be a guest at his or her dinner. Some of the celebrities who participated were Tommy Tune, Julio Iglesias, Zsa Zsa Gabor, Peter Allen, Eddie Albert, Donna Summer, Petula Clark, and Donald

O'Connor. Following the dinners, all the parties converged on the Fontainebleau Hilton on Miami Beach for dessert and a show. Elizabeth Taylor addressed the gathering and presented an award.

Once the group was able to bill it as a night with Elizabeth Taylor, more people begged to be honorary committee members than were needed. Honorary committee members were given specific instructions: They were to host dinners at their own expense, then transport their group to the hotel for the show. Some 1,200 people attended and the event raised $2.2 million.

In this case, the honorary committee played a much more active role than is often the case. But even so, there were many people on working committees who saw to the actual execution of each of the 20 dinner parties and the grand finale at the Fontainebleau. The organization's paid staff and its working committees were responsible for booking the hotel and limousines and arranging for food, decor, lighting, sound, invitations, printing, and publicity.

Every potential committee member should be invited via letter to serve. Figures 4-1 and 4-2 are examples of such a letter. The letter should clearly state what the recipient is responsible for. ("As a member of the committee, you are expected to put together a table of ten friends," or "purchase ten tickets" or "acquire and install all decorations.") Other duties should be clearly spelled out as well. The major role of a working committee—and, in ideal circumstances, the honorary committee as well—is to sell and/or buy tickets to your event.

Each committee should function as a cohesive group with one purpose: making the event a financial success as well as an enjoyable experience so people will want to do it again. This is often a hard balance to obtain. The key to keeping the balance is to have an event coordinator who keeps track of all the tasks of committee members, someone who keeps an eye on the big picture (as explained in chapter 3).

The Boy Scouts always have successful events because they know how to use committees. For a dinner event, each committee member commits to selling (or buying) a table. If a 300-person event is planned, for example, each of 15 committee members buys a 10-seat table and sells another table for 10. That way, the event

Figure 4-1. Sample Committee Invitation Letter from the Transplant
Foundation of South Florida

Transplant Foundation of South Florida

September 21, 1990

Mr. and Mrs. Hans J. Hvide
2550 Del Lago Drive
Ft. Lauderdale, FL 33308

Dear Mr. and Mrs. Hvide:

Patrice Cobb Cooper suggested that we invite you to join
her, and special guest star PHYLLIS DILLER, as a member
of the Committee for **"There's No Business Like Show
Business", Stage II.** This event is sure to be one of the
finest events of the upcoming social season.

This spectacular evening of entertainment, gourmet food,
and dancing will be held on Monday evening, March 11,
1991 in the Great Hall of the Boca Raton Resort and Club.

Committee members will be asked to personally buy tables,
sell tables or help to put tables together for this
benefit. Tables of ten will range from $1,500 for Star
Patrons to $5,000 Star Grand Benefactors. Committee
Members will get special listing in the evening's program
book, on the invitations, and have prime seating!!

We would also appreciate committee members providing us
with a personal mailing list for the invitations.

This event is a major fundraising benefit for the
Transplant Foundation of South Florida. The Foundation
educates the public about organ donation, supports
research, and helps patients with financial needs as
related to transplantation.

Thank you very much in advance for agreeing to work with
us on "There's No Business Like Show Business", Stage II.

Sincerely,

Harry Freedman
Executive Director

HF/pdl

Figure 4-2. Sample Committee Invitation Letter from the 1989 Grand Prix Gala

```
                    GRAND PRIX GALA 1989

                    DRAFT COMMITTEE LETTER


Dear

We greatly appreciate your interest, support and ideas in reference
to the 1989 Grand Prix Gala.

We have enclosed a fact sheet which summarizes the basic
information about the event.  We have also enclosed a list of
Steering Committee members for your use.  The Steering Committee
will be working closely in helping to formulate plans for this
year's gala.  We are planning a second meeting in early January to
discuss a Preview Party for the event and to hopefully announce the
major entertainment for the gala.

We are looking to form an Honorary Committee whose major
responsibility would be to personally buy tables, sell tables or
help put tables together for the event.  All Honorary Committee
Members will be listed prominently on the invitation and in the
evening's program.  Please keep us informed as to those individuals
and corporations that would like to serve on this Honorary
Committee.

Since there are often tax considerations for making donations, you
can feel free to pre-sell tables for the gala.  Please use the
enclosed form to indicate to us table support.

It is most important that we receive your personal mailing lists
as soon as possible so that they can be put into our computer
system and merged with other committee lists to avoid duplications.
Please feel free to contact us if you have any questions or
concerns.

Our best wishes for a happy and healthy holiday season.

Sincerely,
```

quickly sells out. Even if a few people don't honor their commitments, the group must sell only a handful of additional tickets.

How to Get People Involved

Before your committees can work successfully, they must be properly staffed. Assess your board, your staff, and your key volunteers, then figure out where you have vacancies and go after the people you need to do those jobs.

A few ways to get top-notch people involved include:

1. Read the social columns of local newspapers to see who the movers and shakers are, then seek them out.
2. Look for involvement of upper-level management of large corporations or businesses.
3. Be aware of new businesses moving into area that might want to draw attention to themselves. Sometimes the principals will be willing to sign on.
4. Ask key volunteers to bring in friends, business associates, and acquaintances.
5. Look at large service companies—accounting firms, banks, law firms, stock brokerages—for potential committee people because they have large client bases to which they may sell tickets.
6. Seek involvement of other service organizations one of whose major goals is fund raising. A few examples: Junior League, Kiwanis, Rotary, Optimists. These groups are particularly useful in helping to distribute publicity and make follow-up phone calls.
7. Check area high schools and colleges (fraternities and sororities) that might have service groups that would work for you. This is a good way to get young people involved early.

Honorary Committees

Honorary committees are normally groups of socially prominent individuals—business and religious leaders, politicians, so-

cialites, celebrities—through whose participation you will attract
people to support your cause. Generally their role is limited to
lending their name to your cause. In some cases, you might want
to honor a prominent chairman at the event. This encourages the
honoree to invite business associates and friends to attend. Many
honorary chairmen like to be seen in the company of celebrities.

The National Parkinson Foundation frequently secures prominent chairmen because of the involvement of Bob Hope. When
someone like Hope—the king of charitable fund raisers—is involved, major corporate donors line up to be honorees—often
making substantial donations—at the annual Parkinson events.
They know that Hope will present their award—an event that will
be photographed and publicized—and that makes it highly coveted.

Working Committees

Working committees do just what the name implies: They
work closely with the group's paid staff to produce the event. The
responsibilities of these committees often include:

Decorations

This group comes up with the look of the event and deals with
vendors or a party planner to achieve that look. It takes care of
renting tables and chairs, if necessary, and obtains door prizes
(unless you want to give away a great many of these, in which case
it should be a separate committee). These people also are in charge
of assembling and dispensing any giveaway bags guests might
receive. They also sell tickets.

Entertainment

This committee coordinates music or whatever entertainment
is planned, working closely with the events manager to acquire
appropriate talent within the amount budgeted. The events man-

ager usually negotiates the contracts with entertainers. Committee members also sell tickets.

Table or Ticket Sales

Although all committee members are supposed to sell tickets, this group has greater responsibility for sales than the others. The more people you have on this committee, the greater your ticket sales are likely to be. Each member of this group usually commits to buying a certain number of tickets and selling a matching number. They formulate the list of people to whom invitations or notices will be mailed and solicit block purchases from corporations and individuals. A subgroup, the phone committee, does the follow-up phone calls to get people signed up.

Publicity

If your organization is large enough to have paid staff, they normally handle publicity. But, in some cases, a small cadre of volunteers will handle the writing of press releases, research whom to send them to, mail them out, and make follow-up calls. The same person who sends out the releases ought to do the follow-up phone calls. Generally, one or two members serve as liaison people for the media on the day of the event. Members also sell tickets.

Invitations

This can be its own committee, or a subgroup of the decorations committee. The group decides on the design, format, and content of the invitations; negotiates and coordinates with the graphic artist, and printer; and proofreads the invitation before it is sent out. Members also sell tickets.

Food

This committee develops the menu, based on the event's theme and budget. It coordinates with the hotel, caterer, or volunteers who will prepare the food. If your volunteers are purchasing and preparing the food, they may comprise a subgroup. Either someone from this committee or the events manager does the actual contract negotiating with hotels or caterers. If additional kitchen equipment is needed, this group is responsible for getting it ordered, delivered, and returned. All members also sell tickets.

Registration and Check-in

Members of this committee keep track of who has signed up to attend. They also make sure the proper equipment (computers, tables, chairs, etc.) is at the registration site. They determine what to give people as they check in (a program, table assignment card, etc.). They handle the check-in the day of the event. Members also sell tickets.

Program Book

This group decides on the size of the book and what it will look like. They sell ads in the book, write whatever copy is needed, supervise printing, collect money from advertisers, and handle the book's distribution. This should be a big committee; the more people involved, the more ads you are likely to sell. Members also sell tickets.

Special Committees

Depending on the event, additional committees will be needed. An auction will need an acquisitions committee. An arts and crafts or antiques show requires a committee to coordinate the vendors and booths. Consult your checklist to determine whether there are duties on it that do not fit into any of the above committees and, if necessary, form a committee to take care of them.

Depending on the size of your volunteer staff and the nature of the event, you may have as few as two committees or as many as ten. No matter what specific task a committee is responsible for, everyone on every committee must sell tickets.

A member of the working committee should meet regularly with honorary committee members. Though time-consuming, such contact is bound to make the event more successful. Regular contact, for instance, allows the working committee repeated access to honorary committee members' contacts—i.e., the people with the most money. The more people you can approach to buy tickets or underwrite costs, the more money the group will make.

Suppose a businessman just concluded a big deal with a client. When a working committee member talks with him, he is likely to mention it and suggest that the client be contacted to support the cause.

While honorary committee members generally have higher incomes and significant social prominence, working committee members may be more wide-ranging. There might be a socially prominent committee chairman and a number of volunteers from various walks of life.

To make sure working committees are productive, follow these basic guidelines:

1. The overall chairman or staff person running the show needs to divide up the duties of an event among the committees and make sure that each one knows exactly what's expected of it.
2. The overall chairman designates the chairman of each committee in writing, spelling out duties, goals, and budget. Pick chairmen who are tactful, organized, and able to make meetings productive. They must also be willing to finish tasks that their committee members fail to complete.
3. Although meetings are necessary, don't meet simply for the sake of meeting. There should be a purpose to each gath-

ering. Meetings should start and end on time and last no more than an hour. All committee members should be thanked at every meeting. When possible, take care of little matters by phone or FAX. The committee gathers only to report on progress and decide what is to be done next.

All committees must be under the single direction of an events or staff coordinator. Committees left to their own devices can create big problems. It should be made clear to all committee chairmen that financial commitments can only be made by the authorized representative of the organization producing the event.

A case in point: At a Miami Grand Prix Gala dinner for 600, the event planner was surprised to find that the menu had been changed from the agreed-upon chicken dish to a lobster and steak dinner. Obviously, there was a big difference in price. The chairman said she had gotten a local supermarket chain to donate the filet mignons and, as a result, felt the group could afford the change. However, she failed to note that the addition of lobster increased expenses by $6 a person—or a total of $3,600.

TIP: If you are in charge, make sure all vendors know that you are the only person authorized to make financial commitments for the event.

Committee Chairmen's Responsibilities

All committee chairmen should report monthly to the event coordinator. Committees should meet on a regular basis at least once a month until six weeks prior to the event, then at least weekly. All committee chairmen are responsible for giving written estimates to the event coordinator and getting final approvals from that person before committing to them. The committee chairmen come together at least twice prior to the last month before the event for an overview of what is happening and to share ideas.

Relief Team

Events tend to be very labor-intensive. In the last few months before an event, it's always helpful to have volunteers staffing the phones, helping with extra typing, stuffing envelopes and media packets, and helping to follow up loose ends.

If you have an in-house staff, they should be responsible for everyday typing and correspondence, phone follow-ups with major contributors and sponsors, keeping volunteers happy, getting letters out to volunteers, and making sure the event is moving ahead well operationally and financially.

Role of Event Coordinator

The event coordinator keeps track of what each committee is doing and spending. He or she should also retrieve mailing lists from all committee people so the lists can be merged for invitation mailing six weeks before the event. This person should organize committee members to write personal notes to key potential purchasers of blocks of tickets or tables.

Role of Consultants

Sometimes a consultant can help in trimming expenses, come up with additional ideas for revenue, or provide expertise the organization's staff might lack. A consultant's toughest job is to assess the likely outcome of an event and, if it appears that it will be a failure, to advise that it be called off.

All-Out Effort

Three weeks before the event there should be an organized telephone follow-up by as many volunteers as you can muster. They should be calling those who have received invitations but have not yet responded. Try an appeal such as: "I'm calling for Mrs. Jones-Smythe. She's already purchased 10 tickets to this event and she hopes you'll be able to join her. Can I put you down for the same?"

TIP: By having people work the phone the last three weeks, you can often double the number of people who attend.

Mrs. Petry, a prominent socialite, wanted to hold a big event to raise money for a local health-related charity. When the event coordinator contacted her, she informed him she had already sent hold-the-date cards to 2,000 of her "closest friends." When asked who was on her committee, she said, "I don't need a committee. When I invite my friends, they come."

The site for the party held more than 500 people, but only 130 attended the event. Obviously, all were friends of Mrs. Petry. However, if she had had a working committee of corporate and business sponsors, the event could have been far more successful. The moral: No man—or woman—is an island.

Egos

Often events fail because of egos. Too many people insist on having things their way, at the expense of the charity. In creating a fund raiser, it's important that the coordinator take a strong role so that it does not turn into an out-of-control spending spree or clash of personalities.

First-class events can be run without $40,000 in flowers, European china, and free entry for dozens of good friends. It's far better for an event to have raised $50,000 than to break even—or worse, lose money—after six months of hard work by hundreds of people. Everyone needs to feel important, but it is the role of the event coordinator or the executive director to make the tough decisions and stick by them.

Thank Yous and Recognition

Your major volunteers should always be listed on invitations, programs, and, if possible, in some sort of thank-you article in your organization's newsletter or a community newspaper. Special touches go a long way toward garnering loyalty, too. Send volunteers notes of appreciation or small flowering plants or hold a modest thank-you luncheon. This will show volunteers that you appreciate their time, creativity, and, most of all, support.

Committee chairmen should be properly thanked with a certificate or plaque, if possible, along with an appropriate cover letter. It is best to present these tokens of appreciation at the event so those involved can be publicly recognized for their work.

If you have exceeded your goal or raised a substantial amount of money, this should certainly be announced as part of the recognition of the work of volunteers. If there is a suitable place in your organization's headquarters or office, it's a nice touch to display plaques listing those volunteers whose work made your successful event possible.

The Voluntary Action Center of the United Way of Central Indiana found a unique way to express gratitude. During National Volunteer Week (observed in late April) it organizes 50 callers to phone some 3,000 volunteers to thank them for their work that year. The center contacts local companies which supply volunteer callers. Local notables—the mayor, sheriff, and others—also are asked to participate. Two companies donate the use of their headquarters as calling sites, and provide food and phones for the volunteers. Area groups simply type out a list of those they wish to thank and the Thank-a-thon phone team does the rest.

For those individuals who have performed over and above the call of duty or raised substantial dollars individually, you might want to send flowers or a plant at your own expense. This particular attention to detail always pays off when you need to ask for that special favor to work hard again on the next event.

Photography

Photographs from the event should be sent to community newspapers for publication and to key committee people as another form of thank you and as a remembrance.

CHECKLIST

☐ Assess your manpower resources, then figure out how many more you will need, encouraging those already on board to help get others involved.

☐ Organize your honorary committee, confirming each person's involvement and responsibilities in writing.

☐ Organize working committees, confirming each person's involvement and responsibilities in writing.

☐ Have working committee meet once a month until six weeks before an event, then have brief weekly meetings.

☐ Chairmen of each committee should meet with the event coordinator at least once a month up to six weeks before an event, then meet weekly.

☐ Secure volunteers to help with last-minute tasks.

☐ Make sure there are enough people to handle follow-up phone calls in the last weeks before the event.

☐ Remember to thank all committee members at every meeting and to follow up after the event with a thank-you note, plaque, photos, or small gift.

Chapter 5

On Location

It may be that Cousin Melissa had a lovely wedding at that beautiful historic home in the park. And the Goldman bar mitzvah was a smash in an airplane hangar. But in neither case was budget a primary consideration when these well-to-do families planned their little darlings' celebrations.

For a nonprofit group, usefulness, not beauty, is a far better measurement of a site's suitability. It's much less expensive to decorate a room than it is to truck in kitchen equipment, tables, and toilets. When discussing a site, many people will suggest places based on their experiences there. But in most cases, these people saw the site after it was spruced up. They generally have no conception of how much time and money it took to make the place look and function the way it did.

That's why it's up to the event manager and chairman to conduct the research required to make a reasoned choice of locations, rather than acceding to committee members' enthusiasm for a site that may be beautiful but unsuitable for the group's purposes. This means you need not—and should not—automatically look for the biggest, the flashiest, the most expensive spot you can find. Instead, seek out one that can best provide you with the basics at a price that's within your budget and leaves sufficient funds for decorating. Of course, the best of all sites is one that meets all the practical needs of the event *and* has some aesthetic appeal. It may seem like a monumental task to determine which site is best, but a systematic approach will help streamline the process.

Basically, there are four main factors to consider: cost, size, facilities, and location. Take each factor and figure out how it applies to your event and the sites you consider.

First, develop a list of possible sites. Look in the Yellow Pages under churches, halls, caterers, hotels, restaurants, parks, and recreation. In colder climates, add ice skating rinks and ski resorts. In warmer regions, consider public beaches as well. And don't forget the unusual locales, such as farms, caves, and construction sites.

One group that uses out-of-the-ordinary sites to great advantage is The Foundation for Architecture in Philadelphia. According to executive director John Higgins, more than 4,000 people attend the group's annual Beaux Arts Ball, which is always held around Halloween in a building under construction or renovation. The organization uses the money it raises to fund the preservation of historic buildings and architecture.

In 1988, the group held its ball at Wanamaker's, a posh and historic downtown department store. The affair took place on the two spacious top floors of the store, which had been gutted in preparation for renovation to create office space.

The developer, eager for a chance to bring in thousands of people, paid the foundation to hold the event there. The foundation used that money to market the ball. The plumbing and electrical contractors working on the renovation installed toilets and did the necessary electrical work, donating about $90,000 in goods and services.

Other than the basic electricity and some construction lighting, there was nothing but a vast open space with which to work. The foundation added lights, created a haunted house area, a section for refreshments, and a big stage for the costume parade, plus dance areas with different types of music in each. There were huge platforms on which the costumed guests could display their outfits, and closed-circuit televisions so guests in one area could see what was happening elsewhere. The group served dinner to 1,000 people on the 11th floor, then hosted some 4,000 people at the ball and costume parade on the 12th floor.

The foundation mailed out 5,000 invitations. Tickets were $200 for dinner followed by the party or $45 for the party alone. Corporate tables were $3,500 each, entitling the company to ten seats at the dinner, entry to the party, and preview party and listings in the program book. The ball grossed $525,000 and netted $262,000, about a 40 percent return. This was not only a fund raiser, it was a friend raiser as well, because it exposed thousands of people to the group and its work.

While this event works well for the architecture foundation, that does not mean that such a lavish and risky event will work for every group. The Beaux Arts Ball has grown over the years, has built up a following, and has a generous supply of front money. This is the kind of event that could financially ruin less well-endowed groups.

But the lesson here is not to limit yourself to places you'd categorize as banquet facilities; there are all sorts of places likely to be able to handle your event. A few might include: airplane hangars, public gardens, lighthouses, plantations, parks, stadiums, boats, shopping centers, country clubs, schools, and wineries. Consider renting out a whole restaurant—or a bare banquet room—and create a theme if you can't find an appropriate one anywhere.

Unusual sites will vary from place to place, but what works elsewhere might well be adapted to your town. Go to the local library and check back issues of major newspapers (the *New York Times, Los Angeles Times, Chicago Tribune, Miami Herald*). Check the society pages for reports of unusual party sites. Establish a file of such sites for future reference. Another good source of inspiration is *The Fundraising Formula, 50 Creative Events Proven Successful Nationwide* by Katie Kraatz and Julie Haynes.

SITE QUESTIONS

Once you have a list of possible sites, make a basic survey form to record notes from your preliminary phone calls. This form should include:

1. NAME OF SITE
2. ADDRESS
3. PHONE AND CONTACT PERSON
4. OWNERSHIP (PUBLIC OR PRIVATE)
5. DIMENSIONS OF SPACE TO BE USED
6. INDOOR OR OUTDOOR
7. HOW MANY PEOPLE WILL IT HOLD?
8. DATES AVAILABLE
9. COST
10. WHAT'S INCLUDED?
11. EXTRAS (RENTALS)
12. RESTRICTIONS/PERMITS NEEDED
13. AV EQUIPMENT AVAILABLE?
14. KITCHEN EQUIPMENT AVAILABLE?
15. DEPOSIT
16. REFUND/CANCELLATION POLICY
17. ON-SITE CUSTODIANS/SECURITY?
18. STORAGE SPACE AVAILABLE? COST?
19. FIRE STANDARDS? IS FIRE INSURANCE IN-CLUDED IN PRICE?
20. CAN YOU BRING IN THE CATERER OF YOUR CHOICE OR IS THERE AN APPROVED LIST (hotels, of course, will not allow outside caterers in)?
21. REFERENCES

Contact each establishment by phone and ask for this information. Strike from the list any sites that are too small, too large, too expensive, or too booked up. Once you've narrowed it down to two or three possibilities, ask the manager for the names and telephone numbers of other organizations that have held affairs there. Contact someone from each group to find out how the events turned out, how well the site met their needs, what shortcomings or strengths they discovered.

Cost

How much can you afford to spend (refer back to the budget worksheet you completed in chapter 2)? When figuring out the cost of a site, make sure you take into consideration what else you will need if you rent it. For example, you may find a lovely hall, but it might not have enough chairs and tables, kitchen facilities, or bathrooms. If you have to rent these in addition to the room, the cost of using this site rises. (This is especially true of outdoor sites, whose base rental price will usually be lower than an indoor site, but for which you will have to rent many items that are part of the rental of a hotel ballroom or banquet hall.)

Besides determining a site's suitability, make sure to find out how much set-up time you will be allowed. It can take several hours to prepare a room for an event (setting up tables, chairs, dishes, decor, and staging). Make sure you'll have access to the room in time and what additional costs might be involved.

TIP: Find out who will be using the room before you and what decor they plan. Ask them to donate their decorations to your group.

When the University of Miami/Jackson Memorial Burn Center held an event, it saved a bundle by holding the affair in a room used the previous day for a convention dinner of the National Basketball Association. When asked, NBA officials readily agreed to donate the $20,000 worth of decor. In addition to the money the burn center saved, no one from the group had to spend any time decorating.

For some events, such as fashion shows, you may need a full day to set up. In these cases, it may be necessary to reserve the room for the whole day. The establishment may charge extra for tying the room up that long, although some may raise the price of the food instead.

Size

Room size is the trickiest part of site selection. The type of event you plan plays a big role in determining the size site you need. The amount of space needed to hold 200 people for a cocktail party will be considerably smaller than what's required for a sit-down dinner for the same group. If the crowd just fit into the room last year and you are adding a fashion or stage show this time, you will need a larger space.

Make a list of activities, then mentally walk through the event. Where will the registration table go? Where will people have cocktails? Eat dinner? Where will the stage be? Where will the actors dress? Will there be a reception line? If so, where will it form?

TIP: Don't rely on the figures given by the site management. The per person space allowance may not be adequate for the type of event you plan.

Measure the site. Multiply the length by the width to get the total square footage. Subtract space for areas that block views or impede traffic.

How much room is enough? For stand-up buffets and receptions, figure on 8 to 10 square feet per person. For a show in a theater or auditorium, plan on 10 to 12 square feet per person. For a seated banquet, you need about 12 square feet per person. If you plan dancing as well, add two square feet per person. For meals in tents don't forget space for the kitchen and prep tents. For parking, figure on about half as many spaces as people you expect. There should be one valet per every 25 cars.

TIP: For outdoors sites, visit after a heavy rain to check for flooding. If you plan to erect a tent, make sure the ground will support the tent anchors.

Facilities

Picking a site can be like buying a dress or suit: At first glance, you may love the look of it so much, you are apt to overlook a less-than-perfect fit. But the first time you wear it in public, you notice all its flaws. A site that looks good but doesn't quite fit your event can be far more disastrous. While you want it to be attractive, remember that your decorations committee can do much to spif up a less-than-visually-perfect site. What you must have are some basic necessities, such as adequate parking, enough space for the number of people expected to attend, sufficient kitchen and bathroom facilities, and staff.

In considering an outdoor site, remember that you can end up spending thousands of dollars bringing in things such as toilets, electricity, lights, sound equipment, and maybe a tent. Then, after you have gone to the added expense, you are still dependent on the whims of nature to provide good weather. Such considerations are why more than two-thirds of events are held in hotels, halls, or churches.

When the Florida South Chapter of the American Society of Interior Designers decided to hold a benefit, the committee came up with "A Designers Weekend" at an area racetrack. The weekend-long event would include tents in which designers would each create a room or setting. There would be a cocktail reception to kick it off, races, food booths, a program book, and a dinner Saturday night, with a celebrity entertainer, all in big tents.

When the group drew up its initial budget, it totaled $292,500, not counting wine and liquor, which the committee hoped to have donated. The budget accounted for most of the anticipated expenses, including the rental of all the equipment that would have had to be brought to the site. The group expected to gross $465,500, which meant it would raise $173,000—not a great fund-raising effort even on paper. That's assuming 900 people paid $250 to $500 each to have dinner under a tent at a racetrack. (Established events in the city charging a maximum of $250 often could not attract 900 people.)

The other expense not figured in was the cost of bringing in a star's staff and musicians. By the time everything was added up, it looked as if this was going to be a very time-consuming event to pull off—and a money-loser, too. The main problem: The location didn't have adequate facilities for the type of activities the group planned.

When the event manager contacted the Hotel Inter Continental's catering director and he was able to make space at the hotel on the weekend the group wanted to hold its event, he booked the event into the hotel. Instead of tents, the huge atrium lobbies of the hotel and its adjacent office building held the cocktail reception, designers' areas, food booths, and, later, dinner for 700 people. Following dinner, everyone moved into a ballroom for a show featuring Delta Burke as the master of ceremonies and entertainers Peter Allen and Bonnie Pointer (of the Pointer sisters). The event cost much less to stage in the hotel, and the group made a $25,000 profit. Had it held to its original plan and site, the odds were good that the event would have lost money.

Besides the primary site at which the event occurs, most events require additional space, such as a registration area, a place to prepare food and another to serve it from, perhaps a spot for a piano or combo to perform during cocktails.

And then there are the general convenience factors: Where will the event be in relation to a coatroom and restrooms? At outdoor events, you are apt to have to bring portable facilities in.

Location

In most cases, your guests will drive to the event. When considering a site, think about how easy it is to find. If it is an evening event, will they feel safe driving there at night? Is there adequate parking close to the building?

Setting Sites

After phoning the site managers and checking with the references provided, it should be fairly easy to come up with the top three. The events manager or chairman or both should then inspect the sites, particularly the kitchen, ballroom, and parking facilities. Talk with the banquet manager to determine whether you feel comfortable working with him or her.

Once you're fairly sure of a site, arrange to get a copy of the site plan from the facility so that you can map out how you plan to use it. Most ballrooms already have pre-set table plans—those used successfully at previous buffets, fashion shows, and such. Ask for them if they aren't offered.

If you aren't working with a hotel and there isn't a selection of room setups, you likely will have to draw up your own plan. First, create a site plan, mapping entrances and exits, light switches, sound system controls, bathrooms, coatroom, first-aid area, trash dumpster, and parking. You will want to consider which events will take place and how traffic should flow. When possible, arrange to observe a similar event at the site before yours takes place. Sometimes, walking through the event in the room when it's empty can help you determine what goes where.

Sometimes the place just won't accommodate everything in one spot. If you don't have one room big enough for everything, figure out a way to use a number of sites to arrange several small dining areas, with food set up in another spot, entertainment in yet a third.

Once you know what you plan to do with the space, make sure it's all spelled out in the contract you sign before paying a deposit and sending out invitations.

CHECKLIST

- ☐ Develop a list of potential sites.
- ☐ Create site survey form.
- ☐ Contact each site and collect information.
- ☐ Ask for and check recommendations.
- ☐ Narrow field to the top three choices.
- ☐ Visit each site.
- ☐ Check for its suitability in cost, size, facilities, and location.
- ☐ Negotiate the contract; stipulate everything in writing.
- ☐ Sign the contract.

Chapter 6

Reaching for the Stars

Bringing celebrities to town for your special event can be a dazzling way to attract attention and money, drawing in people who may not previously have been aware of your cause. But it can also cause a disaster of stellar proportions should something go wrong. Before deciding on a celebrity event, take into consideration the myriad hidden costs and requirements attached. It may be worth the extra effort, but remember that star power can create magic—or a black hole where your budget used to be.

Hidden Costs

Take, for example, the experience of a chairman in charge of a major benefit for the American Cancer Society. She lined up Joan Collins, known best for her portrayal of the nasty Alexis on "Dynasty." The chairman had done her homework and made arrangements through the publicist who handles "Dynasty." The chairman wanted Collins to attend the party and meet the guests. All the arrangements were made by phone with the publicist. Then the chairman followed up the phone calls with a letter to the publicist, thanking her for making the arrangements for Collins's appearance. That's where she made her first mistake.

TIP: Don't rely on agreements made by phone or informal note. Get them in writing, using the same contracts stars use for paid engagements or, at the very least, a formal and detailed letter of agreement. Figures 6-1 and 6-2 are sample letters requesting contracts for the services of Roberta Flack and Leslie Uggams.

Stars normally have 20- to 30-page contracts, which include riders listing their individual requirements for appearance. Stars' contracts include such things as the way they must travel (usually first class), their accommodations (usually a suite), how many people travel in their entourage (anywhere from one to 30, including makeup artists, hairdressers, personal valets, musicians, tour managers, and assorted groupies), the entourage's travel and lodging requirements, what meals must be provided and what foods should be served, cancellation clauses, and anything else the star requires. Figure 6-3 includes a contract and riders for Lionel Hampton to appear in concert.

In this case, the publicist told the chairman that Collins would require first-class plane tickets for herself and her staff of two, and that she must be supplied with a least $1 million worth of diamond jewelry to wear on the night of her appearance. Thinking this would be a prime promotional opportunity for a local jeweler, the chairman readily agreed. Planning continued on schedule, with Collins's name printed prominently on invitations and news releases.

Two weeks before the event, the chairman called to make sure Collins had received her tickets and information. This time, she spoke with the star's personal secretary, who told her that Collins expected to take at least one piece of jewelry home as payment for wearing the jewels for the evening. The chairman was flabbergasted, saying she understood the items were only to be lent for the evening. The secretary informed her that Collins probably would not attend if she did not receive a piece of jewelry. The chairman convinced a local jeweler to make the donation, the star showed up, and disaster was narrowly averted.

Figure 6-1. Sample Contract Request Letter (for Roberta Flack)

UNIVERSITY OF
SCHOOL OF MEDICINE

January 19, 1989

Mr. Milt Suchin
The Milton B. Suchin Co.
201 N. Robertson Blvd., Suite A
Beverly Hills, CA 90211

Dear Milt:

This letter authorizes you to proceed towards contract for ROBERTA FLACK IN CONCERT.
Ms. Flack would perform with her musicians on Friday, March 3, 1989 at approximately 10:00
p.m., in the Main Ballroom of the Omni International Hotel, Miami, Florida.

This Gala evening is a benefit for the University of Miami/Jackson Memorial Burn Center, The
Mailman Center for Child Development and The Learning Experience School, and is the kick-off
event for the Miami Grand Prix. The Grand Prix Gala, which is attended by approximately
1,000 people, has become recognized as one of the premiere international events of the Miami
social season.

We would like to make an offer not to exceed Twenty-five Thousand Dollars ($25,000), which
would include the services by Ms. Flack and her musicians as a self-contained act. We would
expect Ms, Flack to perform for a minimum of one hour; there will be no opening act. The
Twenty-five Thousand Dollars ($25,000) offer is for Ms. Flack and her musicians only. We
would be responsible for providing appropriate air transportation for her musicians and support
personnel, not to exceed 16 people (2 first-class, 14 coach). We would also provide first-class
accommodations at the Omni International Hotel (1 suite, 15 singles), as well as sound and lights
as appropriate within the Ballroom setting of the Hotel.

We would certainly also like to explore the possibility of having the opportunity of promoting
Ms. Flack's new album in conjunction with the Grand Prix Gala and Grand Prix Weekend. We
certainly would be delighted to have her participate as Grand Prix Marshall prior to the Grand
Prix race on Sunday, March 5, 1989.

I look forward to an early response so we may begin to publicize Ms. Flack's participation in
the appropriate manner.

Sincerely,

Harry A. Freedman
Coordinator - Grand Prix Gala

Office of Development for Medical Affairs
P.O. Box 016960 (R100)
Miami, Florida 33101
(305) 547-6256

Figure 6-2. Sample Contract Request Letter (for Leslie Uggams)

PLEASE FAX IMMEDIATELY - FAX NUMBER: (202) 638-3055

PHONE NUMBER: (202) 347-7469

ENTERTAINMENT OFFER HELPING HANDS AWARDS

Mr. Ed Yoe
Ray Block Productions, Inc.
Director of Talent Buying
666 - 11th Street
Suite 1002
Washington, D.C. 20001

Dear Mr. Yoe:

This letter authorizes you to proceed towards contract for LESLIE UGGAMS IN CONCERT. Ms. Uggams would perform with our EIGHT musicians on Saturday, April 20, 1991 at approximately 9:00 P.M. This event is being held at the Omni Hotel (location) in Miami, Florida.

The Helping Hands Awards is a special recognition evening for major volunteers that support the over 50 charities that support programs and services at the University of Miami School of Medicine. Over 700 people are expected to attend. In past years entertainers such as Phyllis Diller, Connie Francis, Lorenzo Lamas, Bill Harris and Estelle Getty have served as master of ceremonies and entertainers for this prestigious event.

We would like to make an offer not to exceed Eight Thousand Dollars ($8,000) which would include the performance by Ms. Uggams only. We would be providing eight required musicians. We would expect Ms. Uggams to perform for 45 to 55 minutes; there will be no opening act.

We would be responsible for providing two (2) first class tickets for Ms. Uggams and six (6) coach seats round trip for key musicians and staff. We would also provide one suite and six single for up to three (3) days and two (2) nights at the hotel the event is being held at.

We would also provide staging sound, lights and technicians as appropriate within the Ball Room setting for the hotel.

We look forward to an early response so that we may begin to publicize Ms. Uggams participation in an appropriate manner.

Sincerely,

Harry Freedman

Figure 6-3. Sample Contract and Riders (for Lionel Hampton)

AMERICAN FEDERATION OF MUSICIANS OF THE UNITED STATES AND CANADA

(HEREIN CALLED "FEDERATION")

CONTRACT

(Form TP-2)

FOR TRAVELING ENGAGEMENTS ONLY

Whenever The Term "The Local Union" Is Used In This Contract, It Shall Mean The Local Union Of The Federation With Jurisdiction Over The Territory In Which The Engagement Covered By This Contract Is To Be Performed.

THIS CONTRACT for the personal services of musicians on the engagement described below is made this ____4th____ day of NOVEMBER, 19__88__ between the undersigned purchaser of music (herein called "Purchaser") and the undersigned musician or musicians.

Name and Address of Place of Engagement: LUMMUS PARK OCEAN DRIVE & 14th STREET, MIAMI, FL

Name of Band or Group: __LIONEL HAMPTON & HIS BAND__

Number of Musicians: _____   Number of Vocalists: _____

2. Date(s) of Engagement; daily or weekly schedule and daily clock hours:
SUNDAY, JANUARY 15, 1989   2:00 P.M. - 4:00 P.M.

3. Type of Engagement (specify whether dance, stage show, banquet, etc.): __CONCERT__

4. Compensation Agreed Upon: $10,000.00 TEN THOUSAND DOLLARS, PLUS 2 MINI SUITE & 6 DBL. RMS., 2 FIRST CLASS ROUND TRIP TICKETS & 11 ROUND TRIP COACH FARES TICKETS. PLUS GROUND TRANSPORTATION PICK UP AT AIRPORT TO HOTEL & RETURN TO AIRPORT.
(Amount and Terms)

5. Purchaser Will Make Payments As Follows: 50% DEPOSIT UPON SIGNING OF CONTRACT BALANCE DUE IN CASH OR CERTIFIED CHECK NIGHT OF ENGAGEMENT. *(Specify when payments are to be made)*

6. No performance on the engagement shall be recorded, reproduced or transmitted from the place of performance, in any manner or by any means whatsoever, in the absence of a specific written agreement with the Federation relating to and permitting such recording, reproduction or transmission.

7. It is expressly understood by the Purchaser and the musician(s) who are parties to this contract that neither the Federation nor the Local Union are parties to this contract in any capacity except as expressly provided in 6 above and, therefore, that neither the Federation nor the Local Union shall be liable for the performance or breach of any provision hereof.

8. A representative of the Local Union, or the Federation, shall have access to the place of engagement covered by this contract for purposes of communicating with the musician(s) performing the engagement and the Purchaser.

9. The agreement of the musicians to perform is subject to proven detention by sickness, accidents, riots, strikes, epidemics, acts of God, or any other legitimate conditions beyond their control.

(Continued on reverse side)

IN WITNESS WHEREOF, the parties hereto have hereunto set their names and seals on the day and year first above written.

ART DECO/HARRY FREEDMAN | LIONEL HAMPTON

Print Purchaser's Full and Correct Name | Print Name of Signatory Musician   Home Local Union No.
(If Purchaser is Corporation, Full and Correct Corporate Name)

X _____ Signature of Purchaser (or agent thereof) For ART DECO Realty | _____ Signature of Signatory Musician

57-23 N. NEW RIVER CANAL | 1995 BROADWAY
Street Address | Musician's Home Address

PLANTATION, FLA. | NEW YORK, NEW YORK 10023
City   State   Zip Code | City   State   Zip Code

305-547-6256 | 212-787-1222
Telephone | Telephone

_____ Agreement No. | Address to Which Official Communications Should be Sent to Signatory Musician

___RATION OF MUSICIANS OF THE UNITED STATES AND CANADA

(HEREIN CALLED "FEDERATION")

CONTRACT
(Form C-1)

Whenever The Term "The Local Union" Is Used In This Contract, It Shall Mean The Local Union Of The Federation With Jurisdiction Over The Territory In Which The Engagement Covered By This Contract Is To Be Performed.

THIS CONTRACT for the personal services of musicians on the engagement described below is made this __19th__ day of __OCTOBER__, 19_83_, between the undersigned purchaser of music (herein called "Purchaser") and the undersigned musician or musicians.

1. Name and Address of Place of Engagement: NATIONAL PARKINSON FOUNDATION, INC. 1501 N.W. 9th AVENUE BOB HOPE ROAD, MIAMI, FLA. 33136

   Name of Band or Group: LIONEL HAMPTON AND HIS ORCHESTRA

   Number of Musicians: 17

2. Date(s), Starting and Finishing Time of Engagement: MONDAY, FEBRUARY 27th 1984 "STOMPIN' AT THE BREAKERS" THE BREAKERS, PALM BEACH, FLORIDA

3. Type of Engagement (specify whether dance, stage show, banquet, etc.): Stage Show and Dancing (minimum playing time four (4) hours plus one (1) hour rehersal.

4. Compensation Agreed Upon: $10,000.00 PLUS ONE SUITE AND TEN DOUBLE ROOMS PLUS TRANSPORTATION FROM HOTEL TO ENGAGEMENT AND TO AIRPORT

5. Purchaser Will Make Payments As Follows: PAYMENT AT CONCLUSION OF ENGAGEMENT IN THE EVENT OF OVERTIME, THE RATE (Specify when payments are to be made) WILL BE $1,000 PER HOUR.

6. No performance on the engagement shall be recorded, reproduced or transmitted from the place of performance, in any manner or by any means whatsoever, in the absence of a specific written agreement with the Federation relating to and permitting such recording, reproduction or transmission. This prohibition shall not be subject to the arbitration provisions set forth in 7 below and the Federation may enforce this prohibition in any court of competent jurisdiction.

7. Breach of Contract — Arbitration of Claims:

   (a) It is expressly understood by the Purchaser and the musician(s) who are parties to this contract that neither the Federation nor the Local Union are parties to this contract in any capacity except as expressly provided in 6 above and, therefore, that neither the Federation nor the Local Union shall be liable for the performance or breach of any provision hereof.

   (b) This contract, and the terms and conditions contained herein, may be enforced by the Purchaser and by each musician who is a party to this contract or whose name appears on the contract or who has, in fact, performed the engagement contracted for (herein called "participating musician(s)"), and by the agent or agent(s) of each participating musician, including the Local Union.

   (c) All claims and disputes which may arise between the Purchaser and the participating musician(s) regarding the application or interpretation of any of the terms or conditions of this contract, including any disputes between the parties as to their respective obligations and responsibilities hereunder, shall be referred exclusively to binding arbitration. If a claim or dispute involves participating musician(s) who are all members of the Local Union, then such claim or dispute shall be referred to the Executive Board of the Local Union. All other claims or disputes arising under this contract between the Purchaser and participating musician(s) shall be referred to the International Executive Board (herein called "IEB") of the Federation for arbitration and determination in New York, New York. The IEB shall decide any question of whether it or the Local Union Executive Board has jurisdiction over a particular claim or dispute.

   (d) This contract, and all arbitration proceedings conducted hereunder, shall be governed and enforced under the laws of the State of New York notwithstanding the forum or jurisdiction in which an action concerning this contract may be brought. All arbitration proceedings conducted hereunder by the IEB shall be conducted according to the Rules of Practice and Procedure of the IEB which may from time to time be in effect. All arbitration proceedings conducted by the Local Union shall be conducted according to Rules adopted by the Local Union. A copy of the IEB Rules of Practice and Procedure may be obtained from the Secretary-Treasurer of the Federation in New York City, New York. A copy of the Rules of the Local Union may be obtained from the Secretary of the Local Union. All rulings and awards made by the IEB in arbitration hereunder shall be final and binding upon the Purchaser and participating musician(s).

   (e) Except awards of the IEB made on appeal as provided in (f) below, a Purchaser or participating musician, or the agent of any participating musician, may bring an action to confirm or to reduce to judgment an arbitration award of the IEB only in the courts of the State of New York; and the Purchaser and participating musician(s) agree to submit to the jurisdiction of the appropriate courts of the State of New York for that purpose. Should a court of competent jurisdiction in New York confirm or enter judgment upon an award of the IEB, the Purchaser and participating musician(s) expressly agree that the prevailing party in the arbitration award shall be additionally entitled to judgment for reasonable attorneys' fees incurred in enforcing the award in the amount of ten percent (10%) of the award plus court costs therefor. A judgment confirming an IEB arbitration award, for attorneys' fees, and for costs may be enforced in the courts of any jurisdiction in which a party to this contract either resides or maintains an office or place of business.

   (f) All rulings and awards made by the Local Union in arbitration hereunder may be appealed to the IEB by any party who was a participant therein. Appeals from such proceedings shall be perfected in the manner provided in the Rules of Practice and Procedure of the IEB. All rulings and awards made by the Local Union in arbitration which are not appealed to the IEB shall be final and binding upon the Purchaser and participating musician(s). Any party to an arbitration proceeding before the Local

(Continued on reverse side)

FORM C-1 5-79   ::

Lionel Hampton Enterprises Inc.

1995 BROADWAY, NEW YORK, N.Y. 10023 • (212) 787-1222-3

LIONEL HAMPTON
PRESIDENT

BILL TITONE
VICE-PRESIDENT

THIS RIDER FORMS PART OF THE ANNEXED A.F. OF M. CONTRACT.

1. The Producer has the right to cancel this engagement upon written
    notice to the Establishment at least four (4) weeks prior to the
    date of the commencement of the engagement, if the Producer enters
    into a contract prior to such four (4) week period for the services
    of the Orchestra in motion pictures or in a commercial radio and/or
    television series and/or show.

2. The Establishment shall not schedule interviews, personal appearances,
    etc., for the Leader and/or the Orchestra unless specific permission
    is obtained from the Producer through Lionel Hampton Enterprises, Inc.,
    (this provision is necessary due to the fact that travel time into
    this date does not always make appearances or interviews possible
    without undue hardship to the Artist). In order to insure a good
    performance, the Orchestra and Leader need a certain amount of rest.
    Also, the Establishment shall not use the Leader and/or the Orchestra
    for radio or television broadcasts unless specific permission is
    obtained from the Producer.

3. The Establishment agrees to furnish at its own expense the following,
    all of which must be in first-class condition:

        (a) Thirteen microphone P.A. System
        (b) Baby grand piano tuned to 440-A pitch
        (c) Setting up and covering platforms and fourteen (14) chairs on stage
        (d) Proper lighting on stage

4. In order to afford the Establishment the fullest advantage of the
    Orchestra, it is earnestly requested that the Establishment provide a
    bandstand which meets the specifications provided on the bandstand plot.

5. The Establishment shall, at its own expense, provide adequate dressing-
    room facilities at or near the premises to enable the musicians and
    vocalist (if any) to change prior to and following the performance.

ESTABLISHMENT (SIGN HERE)

NATIONAL PARKINSON FOUNDATION
                           INC

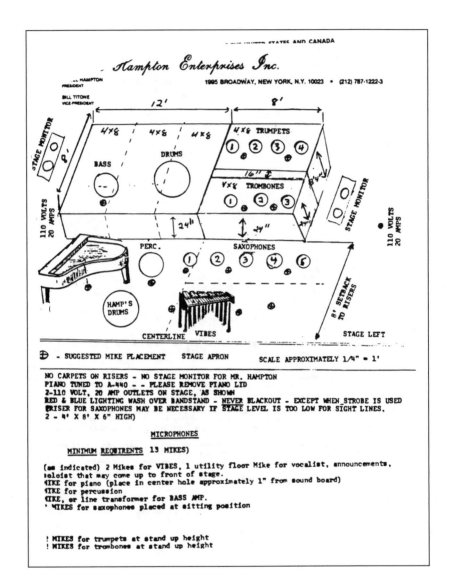

_____ UNITED STATES AND CANADA

Hampton Enterprises Inc.

__ HAMPTON
PRESIDENT

1995 BROADWAY, NEW YORK, N.Y. 10023 • (212) 787-1222-3

BILL TITONE
VICE-PRESIDENT

⊕ - SUGGESTED MIKE PLACEMENT   STAGE APRON   SCALE APPROXIMATELY 1/4" = 1'

NO CARPETS ON RISERS - NO STAGE MONITOR FOR MR. HAMPTON
PIANO TUNED TO A-440 - - PLEASE REMOVE PIANO LID
2-110 VOLT, 20 AMP OUTLETS ON STAGE, AS SHOWN
RED & BLUE LIGHTING WASH OVER BANDSTAND - NEVER BLACKOUT - EXCEPT WHEN STROBE IS USED
RISER FOR SAXOPHONES MAY BE NECESSARY IF STAGE LEVEL IS TOO LOW FOR SIGHT LINES.
2 - 4' X 8' X 6" HIGH)

MICROPHONES

MINIMUM REQUIRENTS 13 MIKES)

(as indicated) 2 Mikes for VIBES, 1 utility floor Mike for vocalist, announcements,
soloist that may come up to front of stage.
MIKE for piano (place in center hole approximately 1" from sound board)
MIKE for percussion
MIKE, or line transformer for BASS AMP.
' MIKES for saxophones placed at sitting position

! MIKES for trumpets at stand up height
! MIKES for trombones at stand up height

TIP: Sometimes it's better to offer a celebrity a small honorarium or fee, which includes travel costs and other incidentals. Fees are negotiable.

The Cost of a Free Appearance

In many cases, celebrities are generous with their time and will offer to appear without charge. For a big-name star, that might mean a savings of $30,000. Or would it? It's easier—and far less expensive—to have a comedian walk out on stage, have a chef do a cooking demonstration, or a sports figure sign autographs, than it is to bring in a singer or dancer. If the star appears with a 20-piece band, it's likely to cost your group plenty (the going rate is about $50 an hour per man and time-and-a-half for overtime, plus transportation, hotels, food, etc.). Figure 6-4 includes the extra costs for an entertainer's band and entourage. Even though the celebrity is donating his or her time, you still will have to pay the band members to perform as well as to rehearse for three to five hours. Then there are the costs of staging, lighting, sets, and props. Often, that free entertainment ends up costing $10,000 or more. Again, look at the celebrity's contract. In the rider will be a list of requirements for producing the show.

If you've never planned a complicated celebrity concert before (no, producing a school play does not count), spend the $500 or so and get an attorney to look over the contract. Laws vary from state to state, so be careful that your attorney is familiar with entertainment and contract law. It could save you thousands of dollars later.

Lining Up a Celebrity

Assuming you have carefully analyzed your group's budget and know how much you can spend (see chapter 2), you then have to decide whether it's worth the time, energy, and trouble it will take to get a celebrity and whether it is going to attract many more

Figure 6-4. Sample Special Food Requirements for Entertainer's Band and Entourage (for Roberta Flack)

SCHOOL OF MEDICINE

TO: Mr. David Kurland, Director of Catering
         Omni Hotel

FROM: Mr. Harry Freedman

DATE: February 28, 1989

RE: ROBERTA FLACK & PARTY

Friday, March 3, 1989

       9:30 A.M. - 11:00 A.M.   Romley Room

       Juice, rolls, coffee & Tea, Milk for 16 people

       2:00 P.M. Sound Check   Ballroom

       Cold cut platter, rolls, bread, soda, coffee for 20 people

       6:00 P.M. Dinner   Romley Room

       Broiled Chicken, Steamed Vegetables, Side Of Pasta, (sauce on side),
       green salad (dressing on side), fruit salad for 16 people

       9:45 P.M. Pre Show Dressing Room   Romley

       Courvoisier Cognac 1 bottle

       1 fruit bowl

       3 liters of Evian, soda's/diet & perrier, assorted juices, coffee, tea

       napkins, tissue, hot & cold cups, 6 towels

       mirror

Office of Development for Medical Affairs
P.O. Box 016960 (R100)
Miami, Florida 33101
(305) 547-6256

```
2/6/89                    1989 GRAND PRIX GALA
3:25 p.m.

*All persons staying at the Omni International Hotel
```

NAME	ARRIVING (date & time)	DEPARTING (date & time)	Rooms
Flack, Roberta & Martin, Joan	3/3/89 NYC/MIA First Class *****Burn Center/Eastern*********	3/4/89 MIA/NYC First Class	Suite Adj. Single
VOCALS Barnes, Patrice	3/3/89 NYC/MIA	3/4/89 MIA/NYC	Single
Collins, Dennis	3/3/89 NYC/MIA	3/4/89 MIA/NYC	Single
Goodman, Gabrielle	3/3/89 BALT/MIA	3/4/89 MIA/BALT	Single
Jackson, Santita	3/3/89 NYC/MIA	3/4/89 MIA/NYC	Single
MUSICIANS Barnes, Jerry	3/3/89 NYC/MIA Coach **********Burn Center/Eastern*********	3/4/89 MIA/NYC Coach	Single
Bryant, Bubba	3/3/89 LA/MIA	3/4/89 MIA/LA	Single
Hamilton, Phil	3/3/89 NYC/MIA	3/4/89 MIA/NYC	Single
Johnson, B.	3/3/89 NYC/MIA	3/4/89 MIA/NYC	Single
Miles, Barry	3/3/89 NEWARK/MIA	3/4/89 MIA/NEWK	Single
CREW Brown, Randy	3/3/89 NYC/MIA	3/4/89 MIA/NYC	Single
Rubin, Greg	3/3/89 NYC/MIA	3/4/89 MIA/NYC	Single
PRODUCTION Burse, Zola	3/3/89 NYC/MIA	3/4/89 MIA/NYC	Single
Koga, Suzanne	3/3/89 NYC/MIA	3/4/89 MIA/NYC	Single
SOUND Tucker, Al ✶	3/3/89 BALT/MIA	3/4/89 MIA/BALT	Single
PRODUCER Suchin, Milt & Vicki	3/2/89 LA/MIA First Class *********Burn Center/Eastern***********	3/6/89 MIA/LA First Class	Suite
Freedman, Harry	3/3/89 8:00 a.m.	3/5/89	Suite

```
          GRAND PRIX GALA/UNIVERSITY OF MIAMI SCHOOL OF MEDICINE

                        MAGIC LADY TOUR

                   TRANSPORTATION SCHEDULE
                  LIMO SERVICE FOR CELEBRITIES
            * SCHEDULE MIGHT CHANGE IF EASTERN STRIKES
THURSDAY, MARCH 2, 1989


9:00 P.M.  PICK-UP MILTON B. SUCHIN AT MIAMI AIRPORT TO OMNI INTERNATIONAL
           TOWN CAR
           EASTERN FLIGHT #23 LA 1:35 P.M. ARRIVES 9:00 P.M. MIAMI


11:45 P.M. PICK-UP MILTON B. SUCHIN AT OMNI INTERNATIONAL TO MIAMI AIRPORT
           MEETING ROBERTA FLACK/JOAN MARTIN-STRETCH
           EASTERN FLIGHT # 415 LA GUARDIA 9:30 P.M.-+ARRIVES MIAMI 12:25A
           AFTER PICK UP RETURN TO OMNI WITH MR. SUCHIN, ROBERTA FLACK. 3/3/89
           JOAN MARTIN.


FRIDAY, MARCH 3, 1988


12:25 A.M.  MIAMI AIRPORT TO OMNI INTERNATIONAL
            EASTERN FLIGHT #415 LA GUARDIA 9:30 P.M.- ARRIVES MIAMI 12:25 A.


            1 -VAN NO SEATS  -  28 PIECES OF EQUIPMENT

            1-10 PASSANGER VAN - Melvin Craig, Koga Suzanne, Miles Barry,
                                 Bryant Bubba, Barnes Patrice, Collins Denni
                                 Goodman Gavrielle, Jackson Santita,
                                 Hamilton Phil, Barnes Jerry.

            1 TOWN CAR    -      Tucker, Burse, Brown

SATURDAY, MARCH 4, 1989

6:00 A.M.  OMNI INTERNATIONAL TO MIAMI AIRPORT

    1 VAN NO SEATS  - 28 PIECE OF EQUIPMENT

    1 TOWN CAR     - Tucker, Burse, Brown, Melvin

    PAN AM FLIGHT # 360 TO NYC/JFK 7:45 A.M.

8:30 A.M. OMNI INTERNATIONAL TO MIAMI AIRPORT
          EASTERN FLIGHT #16 9:35 A.M.
          10 PASSANGER VAN

    1 STRETCH - ROBERTA FLACK/JOAN MARTIN
ON CALL MILTON B. SUCHIN    FLIGHT TO BE CONFIRMED  TOWN CAR
```

people. Usually, the answer is yes, especially for first-time events or those competing with many others for attention.

The next step is to figure out who will best suit your event. There are all sorts of celebrities—local sports stars and media personalities, politicians, famous chefs, artists, actors, authors, directors, singers, dancers. Generally, it's easier to get a local figure to appear at an event in his or her hometown, which also saves money because you don't have to spring for airfare and hotels. But if you want something bigger, say a national or international star, think through the nature of the event and whether the person you are considering makes sense for that event.

When *Forbes* magazine decided to follow me through a first-time event from beginning to end, I got nervous. The event, a big-budget auction, was to attract an audience of social and corporate leaders. The charity was one that provided services for children and the acquisitions committee collected an outstanding selection of items to be auctioned. But to ensure a large turnout of people who could afford the event and spend freely at an auction as well, I knew we needed an extra attraction. I asked Phyllis Diller, with whom I had worked on previous fund raisers, to perform. By hiring her, at a negotiated charity rate, we had the additional special attraction that made the event more glamorous and a financial success.

When considering your choices, keeping the budget in mind is the primary consideration. If you've only got $3,000 for entertainment, Whitney Houston, Cher, the Alvin Ailey dance troupe, and David Copperfield are not realistic possibilities. If you are considering a sports celebrity auction, you could manage on a fairly modest budget by asking a local sports or media personality to be the auctioneer, then requesting donations of jerseys, hats, balls, tickets, etc. from various sporting goods stores or teams.

Even local celebrities often command fees of as much as $7,000 for appearances and endorsements. Musical acts, such as Roberta Flack, Tony Bennett, or Marvin Hamlisch can run from $20,000 to $45,000, (add $5,000 for the travel expenses of staff and key musicians). Comedians like Phyllis Diller, Billy Crystal, or Whoopi Goldberg work within the same range, but incur fewer staff travel expenses. For someone like Bob Hope, the figures can climb to about $75,000 plus expenses.

If you hope to bring in more than one celebrity and your entertainment budget is tight, consider trying to negotiate a "favored nations" clause. This clause ensures that two or more stars who will appear are treated equally. They are paid the same and they get the same accommodations, amenities, and billing. Sometimes you can also negotiate a lower fee because the celebrities want to work together or it's a prestigious event or cause they support.

The American Cancer Society used this clause successfully at a benefit opening of the Hilton Hotel in Miami at which Rita Moreno and David Brenner appeared. Normally, each charged about $17,500 per appearance. The charity had been given a $30,000 budget by the Hilton. By doing some research, the charity knew both stars would already be in town and so offered the celebrities a favored nation contract that would pay each $15,000, plus rooms and airfare for themselves and their entourages. Brenner and Moreno wanted to work together and agreed.

Reading the Stars

Lining up your star requires creativity and research. You are most likely to convince stars to appear at your event if: 1) it's a charity in which they have a personal interest, 2) they are going to be in your area at the time of the event, and 3) you can afford their fee (possibly through corporate underwriting). There are many ways to get this information. Several years ago Marvin Hamlisch appeared at Mount Sinai Medical Center's Crystal Ball. Asked by the *New York Times* why he donated his time and talent, Hamlisch replied, "The truth is my doctor is at Mount Sinai . . . I had this terrible feeling if I said no and God forbid something terrible happened to me on the street and he walked by, he might say, 'Why should I do anything for him? He didn't do anything for me.' "

The most accessible source is television. Watch the talk shows, entertainment news shows, and televised benefits. Stars often discuss their interests and upcoming schedules on these shows.

Read the supermarket tabloids. There may be a lot of "Woman Has Space Alien's Love Child" copy, but these papers also carry lots of stories about charity work celebrities do. These and other papers have written many stories about Dionne Warwick, Elton John, Stevie Wonder, Gladys Knight, Elizabeth Taylor, and Peter Allen, all of whom have taken an active role in AIDS-related fund raising because of the disease's devastating impact on the entertainment industry. Dick Clark works tirelessly for the National Parkinson Foundation because a relative of his has Parkinson's disease. Phyllis Diller is seen nationally in public service announcements for child care, a cause close to her heart. Doris Day and Cleveland Amory are outspoken advocates for animal welfare causes. And, of course, Jerry Lewis, is synonymous with the Muscular Dystrophy Association whose telethon he hosts every year. Celebrity Service publishes a newsletter listing stars who are doing projects, movies, appearances, etc. The service is fairly expensive (several thousand dollars per year), but if you plan a lot of events with celebrities, it pays to subscribe.

Contact local theaters and performing arts centers, as well as civic centers and convention halls within a 500-mile radius of your town. Ask who will be performing there around the time of your event. It costs a lot less to bring in someone from a nearby city than it does from the opposite coast. Ask for the times and days of the performance, then schedule your event around those, if possible. In New York City, a lot of charity events take place on Monday nights because the theater people are off then and so are available for special appearances. Similarly, do not schedule a sports event—or any other type if you can help it—on a weekend when there's a big game.

Harnessing Star Power

One you have determined which celebrities may be interested in your charity and plan to be nearby, it's time to invite them to appear. You could take the usual route and call a booking agent. The agent is a middleman who generally makes 10 percent of the amount he or she books the celebrity for, and so is looking to get the highest appearance fee possible. The agent, in turn, will negotiate with the representing agency for the artist. This agency also gets a percentage, so the agent there will also want to get the highest amount possible. The agent from the representing agency goes to the star's personal manager, who also gets a percentage. At this point, there are three people between you and the celebrity, each interested in making as much money as possible. Those who go this route will pay top dollar.

There are ways to reduce the number of middlemen. First, if someone in your organization knows the star personally, contact him or her and explain the charitable cause you represent. This often works if you happen to know that the charity is one in which the celebrity is interested.

The best route is generally through a celebrity's publicist. Most celebrities have a publicist, someone who tries to generate positive publicity for them. The publicist gets a regular retainer, rather than a percentage of the star's booking. Celebrity Service lists the publicist, business manager (for legal and accounting matters), and agent handling each star.

If a celebrity does not have a publicist, but appears on a network television show, the show will have a publicist. Contact the television network and ask. The publicist can usually put you in contact with the celebrity's personal manager (something like a surrogate mother), who is on call all the time.

There is an organization of personal managers (see chapter 11) that maintains a membership list. Sometimes the agent can supply it. The personal manager is the toughest person to contact. Most rarely return calls to people they don't know. Persistence is generally the key to getting through. Start calling well in advance and leave messages. Call back daily after that. You don't need to be rude. Politely let the person you speak with know you will continue to call until you reach the personal manager.

For most celebrities, you can contact their union, the Screen Actors Guild (SAG) or the American Federation of Television and Radio Artists (AFTRA) (see chapter 11), with offices in New York or Los Angeles, and someone there can give you the publicist's or general manager's name.

TIP: Don't tell the union or trade group you are planning a charity benefit. All they need to know is that you are interested in having the star appear.

Once you find out who to call, make that call count. Persistence is more important than genius; it may take five or six calls to get through. As with personal managers, be polite. Just make it clear you'll keep calling until you get to talk to someone who counts. Remember that publicists and managers may get as many as 500 calls a day, so you have only a minute or so to make your plea. Plan what you will say. Make it concise and state clearly what's in it for the celebrity. If you have done your homework, mention why you know the person might want to help, and that he or she will be in town (or nearby) the day you are planning the event. An example: "I know Paul Newman will be in Miami for the Miami Grand Prix. I'd like him to attend a cocktail party for the Burn Center, a cause I know he would support, being a race-car driver. I do not want him to perform and it will be positive publicity for him. The charity will provide transportation and security."

Once you have gotten a verbal commitment, follow it up with a letter of agreement, or ask for a written contract. Check the celebrity's standard contract thoroughly. It should state that the celebrity is attending for free (or for whatever cost you agreed upon) and specify who will be paying for extras (travel, room, food, including what will be provided for those traveling with the star). Be specific. If you do not plan to pay for long-distance phone calls, damaged hotel furniture, or room service, clearly state that in the written agreement. Give a copy of the agreement to the hotel front desk and have the general manager sign it to ensure he or she understands what you expect to pay for.

Early in my fund-raising career I made a basic but very expensive mistake by not dealing in writing with the management of a hotel at which we were holding a special event. A few weeks after the event, when the bills came from the hotel, there was an additional bill from room service for $4,000 in champagne and caviar. The charges were made by the back-up singers of the entertainer who had performed at the event. The charity decided to pay these expenses out of the money raised that evening, rather than to harrass the celebrity who had given an excellent perform-ance and had helped to attract a sell-out crowd.

TIP: Be sure that all hotel personnel, including the catering director, front desk manager, and general manager, are informed in writing as to what expenses the charity will pay for.

If musicians are involved, be sure you know what instruments you will have to provide and how many hours of rehearsal time you will pay for. The rider should say the entertainer is responsible for paying for any rehearsal time over the agreed amount.

For newcomers to event production, spending the money to have an attorney review the agreement can be invaluable. Or you might invite a local concert promoter to be on your planning committee to provide such advice.

Once you've lined up your star, you can reduce costs by getting things donated. Some hotels will provide free accommodations; sometimes airlines will cover tickets (make sure these tickets are cancellable and can be changed, because they probably will need to be). A travel agent can be a great committee person and can assist you in obtaining tickets and with complicated travel arrangements for celebrities and their entourages.

Look for local companies willing to underwrite your show. Remember that they will want some benefit as well, such as acknowledgment of their donation in the event program, or inclusion in media advertising.

Like your mother, celebrities appreciate being met at the airport, having their rooms ready when they arrive and at the locations they prefer, and having any special needs dealt with in advance.

When Dick Clark and his wife, Kari, were to be in South America the week before the annual Bob Hope Gala of the National Parkinson Foundation, Kari asked if she could send their formal clothing in advance. I agreed to pick it up. She said they would arrive in Miami at 3 A.M., so no one should bother going to greet them; they'd hail a cab. But because I was familiar with the airport, I knew it would be easier for me to navigate than it would be them, especially after a long flight. I met them, took them right to the limo and on to the hotel, where I'd already checked them in and hung their clothes in the closet. As a result, they were able to get some much-needed sleep before the event. Kari was so pleased, she wrote me a note of appreciation later.

If you handle business with a celebrity in a professional manner and establish a good rapport, you improve your chances of getting him or her to return in the future. Celebrities who are treated well may even lend their names to future mail campaigns and public service announcements. (If you want them to do this, discuss your request in advance with their publicists.)

Remember that celebrities have lives of their own, too. Don't automatically assume that someone who has agreed to appear in a show will attend a cocktail party. If you want them to do that, ask beforehand and make sure it is included in the contract. Some will charge a fee for this.

Even if you have taken every precaution and spelled out everything in the contract, something may go amiss. You have to remember that celebrities, especially big ones, can be temperamental. The University of Miami's Community Alliance Against AIDS discovered this when it staged "An Extraordinary Evening with Sophia Loren." This event, held on posh Williams Island, was a dinner under a tent for 600 people featuring about 30 celebrities, including Julio Iglesias, Donna Summer, Petula Clark, and Donald O'Connor. Loren was the honoree. In soliciting buyers of major donor tables—which went for $100,000 each—contributors were to get their photos taken with Loren. After dinner, the events manager waded through Loren's bodyguards and explained that there was one couple with whom she needed to pose. She refused, saying she was still eating dinner. Later, when the couple was brought over to pose behind her while she remained seated, she deliberately turned so her face wasn't visible. While the donors made their sizable contribution to help the charity, part of their motivation was the picture they had been promised and which Loren had agreed in writing to pose for.

While that's an extreme case, remember when dealing with celebrities that their refusal to do something may not stem from a desire to be contrary, but because people have a habit of mobbing stars, grabbing at them, and touching them. It's understandable that some celebrities prefer to avoid this.

Comedienne Joan Rivers, who stands five feet tall, always gets mobbed by her fans. But once committed to help a worthy cause, there's no stopping her. When she appeared on stage in Miami after attending a crowded fund-raising reception, she quipped, "For those of you who haven't touched me yet, I'll be back down there in a few minutes."

CHECKLIST

☐ Make a realistic entertainment budget including all incidentals.

☐ What type of celebrity can you afford?

Watch television, check tabloids and trade magazines to see which celebrities have an interest in or support which charities.

☐ Check with area performance centers to see who is scheduled to appear around the date of your event.

☐ Schedule event around the celebrity's itinerary.

☐ Plan strategy to invite celebrity. If you know the celebrity, contact him or her personally. If not, locate the publicist.

☐ Make a brief and businesslike proposal.

☐ Follow up the verbal commitment with a written contract or letter of agreement clearly detailing what services you will and will not provide.

☐ Check the celebrity's standard rider requirements carefully (musicians, light, sound, staging, travel, entourage, etc.).

☐ Have an attorney or concert promoter review the contract.

☐ Seek donation of services from hotels, airlines, limousine services, etc.

☐ Look for individual and corporate underwriting.

Chapter 7

Food, Glorious and Otherwise

More than any other single factor, food plays a major role in an event's success or failure, both financially and in the eyes of donors. No matter how spectacular an event looks, if the food is terrible or the service rotten, that's what people are going to talk about—and remember. Food is normally the biggest expense, too, unless you have big-name entertainment, so it is critical to figure out all your options. Failure to do so can result in an event that's memorable for all the wrong reasons.

That's what happened at a $500-a-person benefit for an arts center in Miami. Billowing sheets of white gauze formed a Moroccan–style tent in the hotel's grand ballroom. Mimes in gold and silver paint served as live statues. An 18-piece band played dance music. A classical quintet stood by, poised to play during dinner, which was served at tables agleam with china and crystal.

The organizers of this lavish spectacle took pains to see to everything—they even kept the speeches to less than three minutes each—except the most important one: the food.

First course: a tiny squab, which gave up its life for just a dollop of meat. Next came a poached pear—tasty, but insubstantial at 9:30 P.M. after vigorous dancing and drinking. The main course:

steak au poivre with carrot soufflé. The steak was so tough, it was hard to cut with a knife, let alone chew, and was horribly peppery. The event was saved from total failure by a selection of rich French pastries for dessert. The guests had plenty of room for them. The main topic of discussion at most of the tables was how bad the food was. For all the planning this group had done, no one had conducted a tasting of the food before the event. They took it for granted that at this first-class hotel, the meal would be well prepared. As dozens of diners no doubt told them, they were mistaken.

TIP: Steak is almost always a problem. It can be tough, it's hard to cook to everyone's satisfaction, and it's even harder to deliver hot to large numbers of guests. And many cholesterol-conscious people no longer eat red meat.

There are five main factors that will determine what type of food you serve:

1. MARKET
2. SCOPE
3. LOCATION
4. TIME
5. BUDGET

Figure out each of these factors for your event and your choices will narrow down substantially. Let's take them one by one.

1. MARKET. Who will be there and what are they likely to eat? Women tend to favor lighter fare, while men (especially young men) prefer heartier meals. Older people and young adults often are less adventurous in their tastes, while children are the least accepting of the unusual. Consider dietary restrictions and religious beliefs in planning the menu. Pork chops would offend the Hadassah group; a rich, fatty meal isn't a good choice for the heart-attack recovery dinner; brandied pears are out for an Alcoholics Anonymous gathering. Also consider the group's philoso-

phies: Animal rights activists would be outraged at being served milk-fed veal (or any other meat).

2. SCOPE. Are you expecting 50 or 500? The smaller the group, the less involved planning a dinner will be.

3. LOCATION. Are you planning to serve that group at a church or an outdoor location? Consider what your kitchen facilities will be and determine what is possible to prepare there.

4. TIME. What is appropriate to serve at that time of day? Breakfast usually is the lightest meal of the day, lunch a bit heavier, dinner the most lavish. A buffet can be geared to whatever time of day you hold it. Time of year is important to consider, too. Foods should suit the season. Out-of-season menus can be extremely costly and, in some cases, inappropriate (such as chilled strawberry soup on a wintry night).

5. MONEY. How much can you spend? Are you mainly trying to make friends or money? If you are aiming to make a profit, you have to consider carefully what you spend on food. Don't attempt a steak and lobster dinner if you have a chicken budget. Unless it's a high-priced event or you have a lot of underwriting, choose a moderately priced but interesting meal.

How do you do that? First, think back to events you've been to at which the food was memorable. Talk to friends about their experiences, too, both good and bad. Then talk to the executive directors of the events at which the food was good and inquire who they chose and why.

In shopping around, try out the food in all the places you are considering. Hotels sometimes let you observe other events to give you an idea of how they might handle yours.

When planning a meal, consider what else is going on during the event. A lavish, multicourse meal takes a long time to serve. Consult with the catering manager about how long it will take to serve the meal you are considering. If you have an awards show planned following dinner, you'll want to get the meal over with as quickly as possible and proceed to the program. With an auction, your goal is to make as much money as possible, which means you want to have the maximum number of people there. Serve dinner first and many are likely to leave before the bidding starts. Instead, stretch dinner out and, as soon as people sit down, have the auctioneer start in. Bidding should proceed throughout the meal.

Following are some ideas for food and settings commonly used:

Breakfast

> Country–style—eggs, sausage, biscuits and gravy, grits
> Pancake—pancakes, sausages or bacon, fruit
> Jewish—lox, bagels, cream cheese

Brunch

Most often buffet—two choices each of seasonal fruits, rolls and pastries, two vegetables or salads, plus beef or turkey

Light Luncheon

> Salad with rolls, fruit

Gourmet Lunch

Chilled soup, chicken or veal dish, pasta or fruit salad, rich dessert

Buffet—10 to 12 dishes, including meats, salads, fruit, cheese, breads, desserts

Dinners

Cookout (burgers and hot dogs, ribs, or chicken)
Pig roast
Fish fry
Spaghetti
Potluck or covered dish—divide guests into three groups by last name. One group brings main courses, the next side dishes, the last desserts. Everyone should bring enough for four to six servings; the sponsoring organization usually provides plates, silverware, and beverages.
Sit-down banquet—three to five courses
Buffet—20 or more choices, including meats, salads, fruit, cheese, breads, desserts
Dining galleries—themed buffets
Themed dinner—Chinese, Japanese, Italian, French, Cuban, Californian, Hawaiian, Mexican, seafood, vegetarian, etc.

Miscellaneous

Afternoon tea—finger sandwiches, pastries, coffee, tea
Make your own sundaes

Food as Main Event

Chili cook-off
Pie bake-off
Festival—seafood, watermelon, chocolate, peach, tomato, apple, pumpkin, cherry, etc.
Taste of the town—collection of restaurants offering small samples of their foods
This is just a sample of the types of meals possible. You and your committee will know best what would be most suitable and enjoyable for the people you want to attract.

Sit-Down Meals

Banquets generally consist of three to five courses. Usually, you pick a main course and structure the rest of the meal around it. Whatever your choice, make sure you have some alternatives for those who do not eat meat or are on special diets. Remember, too, that people are more health-conscious than ever before so try to achieve a balance of food groups when planning the menu.

Having an interesting meal does not mean spending outrageous amounts of money. Following are sample menus from David B. Sullivan, director of catering and convention services for the Sheraton Bal Harbour Resort in Miami. How much you spend on a meal will vary according to establishment, region, and specific menu.

Breakfast (averages $9 to $14 per person)

Sample menu at $12 per person:
  Eggs with cheese and chives in puff pastry
  Fresh tropical fruit
  Pear or papaya nectar
  Coffee or tea

Lunch (averages $14 to $22 per person)

Sample menu $18 per person:
  Asparagus spears with chopped egg and French dressing
  Tri-colored angel-hair pasta with sesame seed dressing and
    smoked mahi mahi
  Corn and banana nut breads
  Chocolate-dipped fruits and petits fours

Dinner (averages $26 to $40 per person)

Sample menu at $40 per person:
  Pasta with wild mushrooms and smoked salmon

Rosemary-wrapped rack of lamb with minted sauce
Salad of watercress, hearts of palm, endive, and cherry toma-
toes
Rice with apricots and pine nuts
Artist palette of mousses (strawberry, blueberry, banana) in
chocolate cups with marzipan paintbrush

Buffets

These are the easiest types of meals to serve when you are
faced with a small kitchen; a large crowd; a shortage of tables,
chairs, or servers; or other circumstances in which a sit-down
dinner would be difficult to pull off.

---

*TIP: Don't assume a buffet will be less expensive, especially for a
small group. Buffets are often charged on a 1½ portion per person basis
rather than the single portion per person charged for a served, sit-down
dinner.*

Sometimes a buffet can take longer than a sit-down meal if
you don't have enough stations and it takes people a long time to
get their food. Buffets may also not be appropriate if you have a
very formal affair. Many people do not like to carry food (especially
anything with a dark sauce) across a room when they are formally
dressed. In such cases, consider a modified buffet—in which the
first course (such as salad) is on the table when guests are seated,
the main course is served buffet style, then dessert and coffee are
served at the table.

See figure 7-1 for a sample contract for a buffet meal.

Moveable Feasts

Dine-arounds have become quite popular in recent years. They
can be hosted in several restaurants, hotels, private homes, or a

Figure 7-1. Sample Caterer's Contract Proposal for a Buffet

7/29/86

CATERING

PROPOSAL

NAME: HARRY FREEDMAN

ADDRESS: 150 S. UNIVERSITY DRIVE
                         SUITE F
                         FT. LAUDERDALE, FLORIDA 33324

PHONE: 472-3333

REFERENCE: "FASHIONATION"

DATE OF AFFAIR: FRIDAY, DECEMBER 12, 1986

LOCATION: THE FALLS SHOPPING CENTER

NUMBER OF GUESTS: 800

TIME: 7:00 P.M.

MENU: <u>HORS d'OEUVRE</u> (PASSED BUTLER STYLE ON SILVER TRAYS)

                         MACADAMIA NUT CHICKEN WITH HONEY MUSTARD
                         CELERY BOATS WITH GRUYERE PESTO
                         PATTYPAN SQUASH FILLED WITH RATATOUILLE
                         CARPACCIO ON FRENCH BREAD WITH LEMON MUSTARD SAUCE
                         SMOKED SALMON CREPES
                         A VARIETY OF SUSHI AND SASHIMI
                         CRABMEAT EMPANADAS
                         SCALLOP SEVICHE SERVED IN PETITE ENGLISH CUCUMBERS

                         <u>DINNER BUFFET #1</u>

                         STUFFED LOIN OF VEAL WITH MARSALA SAUCE
                         POACHED SALMON PARISIENNE WITH ROSE AND DILL SAUCES
                         GRILLED MARINATED DUCK SALAD WITH CITRUS MAYONAISSE
                         FRESH GARDEN VEGETABLE MELANGE
                         ORZO WITH HERBED BUTTER AND PINE NUTS
                         FRESH BAKED PETITE PAIN WITH BUTTER ROSETTES

menus continued
on following
page

8944 N.W. 24 Terrace Miami, Florida 33172   Telephone: 592-1311

MENU
continued:

DINNER BUFFET #2

ROAST TENDERLOIN OF BEEF
GRILLED SALMON STEAKS WITH PECAN BUTTER
GRILLED MARINATED DUCK SALAD WITH CITRUS MAYONAISSE
JULIENNE VEGETABLE SAUTE
ROASTED RED BLISS POTATOES WITH CREME FRAICHE
FRESH BAKED PETITE PAIN WITH BUTTER ROSETTES

DESSERT BUFFET

TURKISH MOCHA TORTE
PECAN PIE WITH BOURBON SAUCE
APPLE TART
STRAWBERRY TART
BLACKOUT CAKE
RASPBERRY CHARLOTTE ROUSSE
FRESH SLICED FRUITS
FRESHLY BREWED COFEE AND TEA

CHARGES:

FOOD

Based on 800 Persons:

Menu #1 @ $34.00 $ 27,200.00
Menu #2 @ $29.00 $ 23,200.00

Price includes coordination and preparation of
attached menu. Price is based on a minimum guarantee
of 800 persons.

BAR SERVICE

800 Persons @ $1.75 $ 1,400.00

Price includes mixers, ice, glasses, portable bars
and necessary equipment.

CHARGES
continued:

RENTAL - estimate $ 8,000.00

Price includes buffet/work tables, guest tables, chairs,
linens, china, stemware and flatware. Price is based
on a minimum guarantee of 800 persons.

LABOR

60 Persons @ $13.50/hour
Minimum Estimate - 7 hours $ 5,670.00

8 Bartenders @ $18.50/hour
Minimum Estimate - 5 hours $ 740.00

PORTABLE RESTROOM

Restroom Trailor Rental
  Including Water Standby $ 550.00

mixture of the three. Guests move from location to location for each successive course.

The Make-A-Wish Foundation of Western Pennsylvania raised more than $9,000 with its 1990 dine-around. Six Pittsburgh hotels each hosted one course of the progressive meal. The Sheraton Station Square served wine and hors d'oeuvres, the Hyatt Pittsburgh at Chatham Center served *fusilli al pesto,* the Westin William Penn provided Natchez salad, the Vista International offered filet mignon with pumpkin sauce and goat cheese, the Pittsburgh Hilton served mosaic fruit paté, and the Pittsburgh Greentree Marriott concluded the event with liqueurs, coffee, and more desserts. Participants traveled from hotel to hotel by bus.

In a city in which restaurants or hotels are within walking distance, the cost of such an event would be lower because you would not need the bus. In many cases, you can convince each establishment to donate the food. Because each one provides only one course, expenses are small and, in return, the hotel gets the chance to show off itself and its restaurant to an affluent group of people.

Light Refreshments

Not every event calls for a whole meal. If you are on a very tight budget, or the event is at a time of day when no meal is called for, consider serving a variety of snacks, a wine or alcohol-enhanced punch, and soft drinks.

Any of the preceding options can be successful, if properly planned and executed. Let's go through the process step by step.

Hotel Food

The greatest advantage of a hotel is that it is able to provide everything (food, room, set-up, staging, personnel), while rented halls or other sites generally are not. In working with a hotel, first set up an appointment with the catering director or banquet manager. These people have years of experience in planning events of varying themes for large and small groups.

Carefully communicate your needs: Will guests primarily be young or old? Do they have any religious/health/other food restrictions? Are they accustomed to eating early or late in the evening? What else is planned during the event? How long will it take to serve the various courses selected?

Be prepared with the facts and figures and a reasonable estimate of how much you can spend. It's helpful to give the person a fact sheet about the organization and some specifics about what you hope to accomplish with this event. Such a fact sheet—in letter form—is portrayed in figure 7-2.

You might also ask to have the chef available at the first meeting to discuss menus. Usually, the catering director will suggest a choice of menus that would be suitable for the type of people and event you plan based on your food budget. Be sure to inquire about the way the food will be presented, the size of portions, how long the meal takes to serve, and the amount of service staff available.

TIP: Ask that this identical meal not be served for several weeks prior to your event.

At the initial meeting, finalize the date, which room(s) will be used for the reception and dinner, and how many rooms you will need for overnight guests. (The banquet manager may handle this last issue or suggest you deal directly with the reservations desk.) Ask to visit the hotel to observe and taste the food prior to making a commitment. Before signing a contract, check with other organizations about their experiences with the hotels you are considering (remember the $500-a-plate petrified steak dinner!). And insist on an itemized bid, making sure everything has been covered and there are no hidden extras. Ask if the figure includes parking and extra rooms needed.

TIP: Hotels quote meal cost separately from tax and gratuities (which can add 18 to 21 percent). Other items generally not included: hors d'ouevres and beverages.

Figure 7-2. Sample Fact Sheet

SCHOOL OF MEDICINE

June 7, 1988

Mr. David Kurland
Director of Catering
Omni International Hotel
Biscayne Blvd. at 16th Street
Miami, Fl 33132

Dear David,

I am happy to inform you that we have agreed to hold the Grand
Prix Gala at your hotel on Friday, March 3, 1989. We expect
that, as in the past, this will be one of the premiere social
events of the season.

This gala will attract 600 to 800 of South Florida's most
prominent community and business leaders as well as many
individuals from international companies and the world of sports
and show business.

We are hoping that in addition to holding this important event at
your hotel, that the Omni International Hotel/Continental
Companies can work with us in the following ways:

1.　Provide up to four (4) deluxe suites and
four (4) rooms for celebrities to be used
the weekend of the Grand Prix (Friday,
March 3rd to Sunday, March 5th, 1989).

2.　Underwrite the cocktail reception/preview
party or cocktail reception the night of the
Gala for up to 600 people.

3.　Participation in a Corporate ad in the program
book for the Grand Prix Gala Weekend at a cost
of up to $1,000.

This support is particularly important as we try to maximize
fundraising efforts on behalf of the University of Miami/Jackson
Memorial Burn Center and the Mailman Center for Child
Development, who are the beneficiaries of the Grand Prix Gala
1989.

Office of Development for Medical Affairs
P.O. Box 016960 (R100)
Miami, Florida 33101
(305) 547-6256

Page 2
Mr. David Kurland
Omni International Hotel
June 7, 1988

Other Corporate Sponsors already include Eastern Airlines, which
will be providing transportation for celebrities and
transportation to be combined with hotel space, Miami Motorsports
(Miami Grand Prix), WNWS/WLYF, firefighters in Dade and Broward
counties, South Florida Magazine, several major banks, and many
more too numerous to mention.

The UM/JM Burn Center is one of the busiest Burn Centers in the
nation. Each year in the United States 2.2 million people are
burned, and half of the victims are children. This is a unique
opportunity to help raise substantial funds for a major Burn
Center, which provides service throughout South Florida, the
Caribbean and Latin America.

The Mailman Center helps nearly 6,000 children each year with
learning disabilities mental retardation, physical handicaps or
other disabilities caused by genetics, pre-natal or post birth
damage. In the last twenty years our work in research and care
has won us international recognition. It is your help that is
our hope for the future.

Thank you in advance for your help and support. We look forward
to the opportunity to work with the Omni International Hotel &
Continental Companies for this very worthy cause.

Sincerely,

Harry A. Freedman
Development Director

Ask the banquet manager what the serving staff's standard attire is. If you want something different, expect to pay dearly for it. Most hotels have a standard set of table linens, dishes, glassware, and silverware, too. If you want anything more exotic, it will cost you extra. In most cases, so will candles, fancy candlesticks, and anything else not customarily provided. Your decorating committee or party planner can provide these, so check which would be less expensive.

TIP: If you use rental items, designate someone as a spotter. This person's job is to check items as they are unpacked to make sure everything is there and to do the same thing at the end of the event, making sure everything is returned undamaged to the rental company.

Because use of a banquet room is included in the price of meals, hotels are usually particular about who gets which rooms. Consequently, the larger the group and the more costly the meal, the more receptive the hotel will be to giving you the biggest ballroom. Don't inflate the number you think will come just to get the big room. Remember, an event that attracts 250 people will look like a failure in a room big enough for 500.

Hotels normally require a guarantee, the number of people you expect to attend the event. The hotel also uses this number to determine how much food to buy, how many people will be needed to prepare and serve, and how much set-up time is needed. You normally give a guarantee the week of the event, with a final guarantee 24 to 48 hours before the event. Once you give a guarantee, back it up in writing. This determines how many people you pay for. The hotel will charge you at least for that many and will add on any extras who show up. However, if you guarantee 250 people and only 200 show, you will still pay for the 250. Hotels customarily prepare for 10 percent more than your guarantee so consider that when giving your figure. They also are prepared with substitute meals for vegetarians and others with dietary restrictions. If anything, it's better to underestimate the number you will have attend by 10 to 20 percent.

Most hotels require a 50 percent deposit if this is your first event with them. Organizations that have annual events at a particular hotel may only have to pay 10 to 20 percent. The deposits are usually nonrefundable. Final payment is normally due the night of the event, based on the guarantee, with any additional billing to follow. Most hotels also require you to provide liability insurance.

Caterers

Outside of a hotel, you can get all these services by hiring a full-service caterer. Besides preparing the food, a full-service caterer provides setup, rentals, food, staff, cleanup, and often decor or staging.

Partial-service caterers generally are less expensive than full-service ones, because they don't provide as many services. Among the things you might have to provide yourself would be tables and chairs, tents, cooking equipment, staff, and decor. Remember to add the cost of these things in when figuring your budget.

The least expensive option is a no-service caterer, one who simply prepares the food and drops it off. Who serves it, how, and on what is up to you.

As with hotels, always ask to sample the menu you are considering. Caterers also will require a guarantee for the number of people attending. They usually require a guarantee to be firm at least a week in advance since they need to purchase food and coordinate rental of equipment, tables, chairs, silverware, dishes, etc. They also build a 10-percent cushion into the guarantee for food and rentals.

In addition to charging for food on a per person basis, a full-service caterer also charges for serving staff on an hourly basis, usually with a three-hour minimum. The number of staff is based on the number of guests attending.

David Sullivan, of the Sheraton Bal Harbour Resort in Miami, suggests the following ratio of staff to guests:

- For a sit-down meal: 1 server per 20 guests
- For a buffet: 1 server per 40 guests
- For sit-down or buffet: 1 captain per 250 guests

- For cocktail party: 1 or 2 bartenders per 100 guests, 1 or 2 waiters per 100 guests (depending on how extensive the menu is)

TIP: The exception to these numbers is when the servers are unionized, with rules that require a certain number of workers. These numbers are not negotiable no matter how worthwhile your cause.

There also will be charges for equipment rental (along with a percentage markup for acquiring it for you). Always ask what the markup will be and ask to see the actual rental bill to ensure that you haven't been overcharged.

Get an itemized estimate from the caterer that separates food costs per person from all additional rentals and staff charges. (There may also be a charge for clean-up crews.) See figure 7-3 for a sample catering contract proposal.

TIP: Check with your local health department—or whatever agency inspects commercial kitchens—to see whether the caterer you are considering has been cited for any health violations.

Like a hotel, a caterer will require a deposit (this is separate from the deposit you'll pay to reserve your site) and will have set guidelines for refunds in the event of cancellation. Make sure you know exactly what the cancellation policy is. Be sure that your caterer and event site have coordinated set-up times, clean-up responsibilities, equipment usage, security, and parking. As with hotels, you are likely to be required to provide liability insurance.

TIP: Check your contract to make sure you are not being billed twice for the same items, or charged for rental of equipment that's already on site.

Make sure you ask the caterer what the staff will wear—usually dark pants, white shirt, dark tie. As at hotels, if you want something

Figure 7-3. Sample Caterer's Contract

```
SHERATON BAL HARBOUR        9701 Collins Avenue     Bal Harbour, Fl 33154

NAME: SHORES THEATER/BURN CENTER     FUNCTION ORDER NO:  2142-B

FUNCTION:  LUNCHEON/FASHION SHOW     DATE: THURSDAY, MARCH 15, 1990

IN CHARGE:  MR. HARRY FREEDMAN       TIME:            SEE BELOW

GUARANTEE:        SET:   500         ROOM:            SEE BELOW

        Guarantees must be submitted 48 hours in advance of all functions.
                        (Monday function, 72 hours)

   REGISTRATION/RECEPTION/BOUTIQUE: BALLROOM FOYER/WESTWALL -- 11 AM-12 NOON
             LUNCHEON:  BALLROOM -- 12 NOON - 1:00 PM
                  FASHION SHOW: 1:00 - 2:00 PM
```

BEVERAGES	MENU
	INDIVIDUAL SLICED PINEAPPLE, HONEYDEW, CANTELOPE AND STRAWBERRIES W/YOGURT
WAITERS TO OFFER CLIENT'S DONATED RED & WHITE WINE WITH LUNCH	SALAD NICOISE
CORKAGE: $1.00 PER BOTTLE	GREENS, WHOLE GREEN & BLACK OLIVES, MUSHROOMS, POTATOES PARISIENNE, PIMENTO, GREEN BEANS, CAPERS, TUNA,
SERVICE: $1.00 PER BOTTLE	WITH DRESSING ON SIDE (PRESENTATION TO BE MIXED)
ARRANGEMENTS	ITALIAN BREADSTICKS, ROLLS, CORN AND BANANA NUT BREADS
IN CHARGE OF SERVICE: OSCAR OSLE	LARGE BUTTER ROSES W/LEMON LEAVES
SETUP: ROUND TABLES OF 10, 84 FT RUNWAY WITH STAGE DIMENSIONS TBA. (SEE FLOOR PLAN)	THE FOLLOWING DESSERTS TO BE UTILIZED ON EACH TABLE AS CENTERPIECES: INDIVIDUAL FRUIT TARTS, LEMON & FRUIT
LINEN: T.B.A.	MOUSSE IN CHOCOLATE CUPS AND PETIT FOURS, CHOCOLATE DIPPED TEA COOKIES.
CENTERPIECES: DESSERTS TO BE UTILIZED IN CLIENT'S SPECIAL TRAYS	NOTE: CLIENT TO PROVIDE SPECIAL TRAYS.
PARKING: SPECIAL RATE OF $3.00 PER CAR - INDIVIDUALS TO PAY	CHARGE: $16.00 PER PERSON, INCLUSIVE OF 17% SERVICE TAX EXEMPT: 07-00136-02-23

```
                                      -----------------------------------------
                                                   BILLING
ARRANGED BY:  David B. Sullivan       $_____ DEPOSIT RECEIVED _____
DATE:      2-13-90       (2)           UM-JM BURN CENTER
                                       P.O. Box 016310
                                       Miami, Fl 33101
                                       ATTN: Mr. Harry Freedman  547-6186
```

```
SHERATON BAL HARBOUR        9701 Collins Avenue      Bal Harbour, Fl 33154

NAME:  SHORES THEATER/BURN CENTER     FUNCTION ORDER NO:  2142 - A

FUNCTION:        RECEPTION            DATE:  THURSDAY, MARCH 15, 1990

IN CHARGE:  MR. HARRY FREEDMAN        TIME:          SEE BELOW

GUARANTEE:        SET:  500           ROOM:          SEE BELOW

        Guarantees must be submitted 48 hours in advance of all functions.
                    (Monday function, 72 hours)

    REGISTRATION/RECEPTION/BOUTIQUE: BALLROOM FOYER/WESTWALL -- 11 AM-12 NOON
                LUNCHEON:  BALLROOM -- 12 NOON - 1:00 PM
                FASHION SHOW: 1:00 - 2:00 PM
```

BEVERAGES	MENU

```
2 DOUBLE CASH BARS WITH A TOTAL OF
4  BARTENDERS & 2 CASHIERS TO
SERVE A COMPLETE SELECTION OF NAME
BRAND LIQUOR, MONTEREY VINEYARDS
WHITE & RED WINE & ASSORTED SODAS
TO INCLUDE DIET & PERRIER

LIQUOR:      $4.00                        NO FOOD REQUIRED
BEER/WINE:   $3.00
SODAS:       $1.50

ABOVE PRICES INCLUSIVE OF 17%
SERVICE & 9% TAX

PLEASE WAIVE BARTENDER & CASHIER     -------------------------------------
FEES                                                BILLING

            ARRANGEMENTS             UM-JM BURN CENTER
                                     P.O. Box 016310
IN CHARGE OF SERVICE:  OSCAR OSLE    Miami, Fl  33101
                                     ATTN: Mr. Harry Freedman  547-6186
SETUP: 2 DOUBLE BARS, CASHIER
TABLES, (4) 6 FT REGISTRATION
TABLES SET IN MARBLE FOYER

LINEN:  REG TABLES WITH CORAL
CLOTHS AND GREEN SKIRTING

ARRANGED BY:  David B. Sullivan
DATE:     2-13-90      (1)
```

different to go with your theme, you'll probably have to pay for uniform rentals. Special outfits are generally an unnecessary expense, but there are times when they make a difference.

At a benefit for Health Crisis Network, an AIDS social service agency, a lavish party was held on the grounds of the historic Vizcaya mansion in Miami. The party theme was white. Everything was white, including the tent, the dishes, the guests' outfits, and the serving staff uniforms. If the serving staff had been in the standard black and white, it would have ruined the effect. But when dressed all in white, they became virtually invisible. Food seemed to appear magically before the guests. While such expense is probably out of the range of most groups, this organization could afford spectacular decorations because area businesses, restaurants, and bars donated most of the food and drink.

A benefit for the University of Miami's Burn Center used a less costly, but also effective special uniform for its staff at a formal auction. The benefit used its dalmatian mascot—outfitted in a red bow tie—as the unifying theme on its decorations, invitations, and promotional material. L&M Fashions, a large manufacturer of tuxedos and accessories in Hialeah, Florida, donated red bow ties and cummerbunds for all the workers to wear that night. The people who handled registration, the spotters, and the auctioneers all wore them, making them easily recognizable in the crowd. The chairman thoughtfully gave the events manager a black and white polka-dot bow tie.

Choosing Menus

In deciding on your menu, let the experts help. Banquet managers or caterers design several meals a day for a host of occasions. Their experience can help you or stimulate ideas to make your event unusual. Keep in mind these are only suggestions and you can modify them according to your tastes and budget. In doing so, however, remember that they regularly deal with large groups of people and know how to meet their needs.

There has to be a balance to the menu. If you have a Mexican night, remember that not everyone likes spicy food, so you'll need to have some mild dishes as well. At a Japanese dinner, not everyone will eat sushi, so you should also offer tempura or a plainly cooked fish with choice of sauces for those who like their food cooked. Besides appealing to a broad range of tastes, there are visual and textural facets to consider. Try to design each course so that it has a variety of color and texture.

At a luncheon honoring Gloria Steinem at Philadelphia's Belle-vue Stratford, several considerations shaped the meal. Among them were a primarily female audience, which tends to be diet conscious, and a tight time schedule (two hours for lunch and a speech). Tables were preset with chilled strawberry soup served in a hollowed out coconut atop a bed of radicchio. The main course was medal-lions of veal in light lemon sauce, served with julienned carrots and snow peas for an interesting palette of colors and textures. (For those who were counting calories, there was an option of a Caesar salad with smoked sliced breast of chicken.) Dessert was a ramekin of chocolate mousse surrounded by fresh sliced strawberries along with trays of cookies on each table.

How Much Food?

For a sit-down dinner, figure on six to eight ounces of chicken, fish, or meat per person, perhaps a bit less for banquets. Portion size will depend on your event, too. If it's a dinner after an athletic competition or other strenuous dance, plan on heartier appetites. If the event is lengthy, and dinner will not be served until the end, consider serving a light snack early in the schedule.

On Your Own

Hotels and caterers are not the only ones who can prepare a meal. The final option is doing it yourself or using a group of volunteers. That means you figure out how much food to buy, shop for it, find a place to prepare it, prepare it, serve it, and clean up. You'll still need to rent dishes, tablecloths, silverware, and often the serving ovens and such.

Before shopping for supplies, finalize your menu. Consider your limitations. How extensive a kitchen will you have? How much help and equipment will you have? How skilled is your cooking staff? It's not a good idea to attempt something labor- and space-intensive, such as paella, if you will be working in a home kitchen. When doing your own cooking, try to keep it as simple as possible, using as little equipment as you can. If a recipe calls for stirring until something boils, someone will wind up stirring for ages waiting for a big pot to boil. Don't plan to have fresh string beans or mushrooms, which require individual cutting or cleaning.

If the first *and* second courses need to be served hot, make sure you have enough burners and room to heat both of them on the stove at once. Will you be able to fit everything into the oven at one time that needs to be in there? And don't forget refrigerator and freezer space. Will there be enough room so that all your perishable goods will fit in?

Once you have an idea of what you would like to make, stage a tasting, just like hotels and caterers do. Involve everyone who will be cooking. Try out all the recipes. This small-scale version of your meal will help you work out problems you might otherwise not foresee. Don't get too exotic—tasty, simple fare beats ill-prepared exotic dishes every time.

TIP: Pay attention to the seasonal nature of some foods. Peaches may be inexpensive when you try out your menu in July, but are likely to be astronomically expensive in October, if you can get them at all.

Once you finalize the menu, it's time to make a shopping list. Go through each recipe and list everything you will need to buy. Don't forget cleaning supplies, paper towels, sponges, dishwashing liquid, garbage bags, etc. Figure out what's already available and how to get it to the event site. Then prepare your shopping list. Do your multiplication at home, not in the supermarket aisles. Take your recipes along, too. If you have to pick up more food than you can handle alone, arrange to have two or more people meet you at the supermarket. Shop systematically and always use a calculator to double-check your figures. When possible, go to a food co-op or wholesale discount store to purchase food. Look for sales. Ask the manager whether you can get a discount for large-quantity purchases. If there's a store in your area that's open 24 hours a day, go when it's quiet so you and your six shopping carts do not become a logistical nightmare. Don't buy perishables more than a few days before the event.

There are lots of time savers at your disposal; use as many as you can. Prepare soups and beverages in advance, using about a quarter of the liquid needed. Transport to the event site cooled. Transfer to a pot (or pitcher, for drinks), then add the rest of the liquid. Frozen pie crusts save time in both preparation and cleanup (no pie plates to wash). Pre-sliced meats and breads and frozen vegetables all help cut preparation time.

TIP: When possible, arrange for some food to be prepared in advance at the homes of your cooks. (Do this only with cooks you can trust and whose kitchens are adequate to handle this kind of preparation.)

At the Site

On the day of the event, bring in everything you'll need. If possible, things will have been sliced and cleaned at people's homes prior to being brought to the kitchen. Post the menu, cooking schedule, and assignment of tasks in a central spot where everyone can refer to them. Use the best cooks for the big jobs; let the less culinarily inclined wash dishes and cut fruits or vegetables.

TIP: Place garbage cans or bags in various spots in the kitchen so no one will have to go far to find one. This enables you to clean up as you go.

If Disaster Strikes

Sometimes, no matter how well you planned, something goes wrong. Always have someone taste dishes before they are served.

That way only a chosen few taste failures. But there will come a time when someone uses salt instead of sugar, cornstarch instead of flour, burns something beyond recognition, or simply drops it on the floor.

RULE ONE: Stay calm.

RULE TWO: No matter how desperate you are, don't serve it. Instead, send someone out quickly for some extras to fill in. A few possibilities:

- assorted cheese and crackers
- pre-cooked meats (ham, salami, chicken, turkey) rolled into tubes (cream cheese inside optional)
- assorted fruits (apples, orange wedges, grape clusters)
- quick-cooking rice or pasta
- frozen vegetables (Canned is not a suitable substitute)
- breads or crackers, butter and jam or cheese spread
- trays of store-bought cookies and chocolates
- assorted frozen yogurts and gourmet ice creams

Liquor and Nonalcoholic Beverages

At hotels, you are normally charged per drink or per bottle for alcoholic and nonalcoholic beverages. Most hotels will not let you bring in donated wine or champagne or, if they do, are likely to charge you a corkage fee that can be $2 or more or a percentage of the value of the bottle.

Selection of beverages is determined by the type of event you have, the ages of those attending, and your menu. The first question you might want to ask is whether you should serve alcohol at all. Unless you have a cash bar, alcohol will be another large expense. If you hold the event at someplace other than a hotel and have to buy the liquor yourself, that's a considerable outlay of money. And there's also the potential liability if someone gets drunk at your event, goes out, and runs someone down. More states are passing laws that allow victims and their families to sue not only the person who was intoxicated but whoever served him the liquor, the group that hired the bartender, and the group's board of directors. When you do serve liquor, always try to make sure people do not drink too much and that cabs are available for those who should not drive home. Also, throw out the old wives' tale that coffee sobers you up; it doesn't.

At most fancy banquets, dances, and other such events, it's customary and usually expected that liquor will be available, either at a cash bar or as wine served at the table. Still, at most events there now is an ample assortment of nonalcoholic beers and light alcohol punches as well as wine coolers, spritzers, and just plain sodas and fruit juices. Cash bars are becoming more common, requiring people to seek out and pay for their drinks as a form of limiting intake. It also reduces the number of servers you need. You can keep the cocktail hour short (they used to run about 90 minutes, but most groups limit them to an hour). Skip the after-dinner drinks and the decanters of wine on the table, or close the bar once dinner starts (and count on hearing a lot of complaints).

At some events, certain drinks go with the food served and can be big money-makers. A few examples: beer at a chili festival, Chianti with a spaghetti dinner, margaritas with a Mexican meal. Serve them, but do so in moderation. At sporting events, liquor service sometimes is halted at halftime so that people have a while to sober up before they leave.

There's another good reason to contemplate whether to serve liquor: it's expensive. At a 200-person event, you will need two bottles of wine per table of 10. At $10 a bottle times 20 tables, wine alone would be $400. If people want other alcoholic beverages, the hotel or caterer will probably charge $1.50–$1.75 per drink. The average person drinks two drinks. At $1.50, that's another $600. Then you have to add two bars, bartenders and setups—that's another $300. Already, your expenses are $1,300 just for liquor—more than $6 per person (not including tax and gratuity). A cash bar can substantially offset this cost. By charging $2 per drink, you not only cover the bars, bartenders, and cocktails, but some of the wine as well.

TIP: Sometimes hotels will allow you to bring in donated wine if you have a cash bar. Caterers are more likely to let you bring in your own wine and liquor—it's one less thing for them to worry about.

Soft drinks are necessary even if you serve alcohol. A good selection includes: cola, lemon-lime, and ginger ale, regular and sugar-free, carbonated water, and fruit juices. Other possibilities include fruit-juice spritzers, lemonade, fresh cider, milkshakes, and ice-cream sodas. Coffee and tea should be available, too. At outdoor events, especially when the weather is warm, make sure you have plenty of cold water available.

How much coffee, soda, and alcohol do you need? The general rules of thumb for beverages are:

Coffee: one pound makes about 60 cups
Champagne: one case pours 45–50 glasses
Liquor: one quart makes 25–30 drinks
Punch: one gallon serves 24 cups

In terms of consumption, people generally drink less wine than beer, less beer than soft drinks. For drinks with alcohol, figure about two drinks per person each hour.

A few ways to cut your beverage expenses include:

- Beer costs less in a keg than in bottles or cans. When possible (and practical), consider kegs. (Remember that they can be messy and slow, which may not work well at your event.)
- In getting quotes on hard liquor, ask if the price is based on house brands (the cheapest), name or call brands (more expensive brands), or premium brands. Specify which brands to use and how much liquor should be poured per drink.
- Instead of a free bar, provide two drink tickets per paid guest. After that, guests pay for their own drinks.
- Specify that you be charged based on the number of open bottles of liquor served.

When serving alcohol, keep in mind that there are legal issues to consider, too. In some states, you have to have a permit to hold an open bar. Serving liquor to minors is not only illegal, it will cause many to look with disfavor on your group. And there are the previously mentioned issues of liability in connection with accidents that happen when guests leave your event. Make sure you know what the laws are in your area and make sure they are rigidly adhered to.

Feeding Staff Volunteers

It's best for your staff and volunteers to eat before arriving at the event. It saves time, money, and effort. If they will be there a long time (setting up or cleaning up), you will need to feed them. At a hotel, you can ask if the chef could provide a simple dish and salad in a room away from all the confusion. Another option is to give everyone a small stipend—maybe $5—and let them run out quickly for a bite. Make sure you have beverages (coffee, soda, juice) available throughout the working period for anyone who is helping to set up. It's cheaper if you can provide these yourself (bring them in ice chests), but some hotels won't allow it.

Leftovers

Invariably, there is leftover food. With so many homeless and hungry people, you can often make arrangements to donate it to a soup kitchen or shelter. Hotels and caterers generally won't do this, so you'll need to make your own arrangements, supply containers, and handle delivery. (You can get a receipt from the charity for the donation.) It's a nice touch to mention this in the program or announce it at the event.

Tipping

The general rule on tipping is that 17 percent is added on to your bill and divided accordingly: 13 percent to the waiters and bartenders, 3 percent to captains and maître d's, 1 percent to the catering director.

If people really go out of their way to help with unexpected problems, you might want to give them extra. If the service was excellent and you think you might want to hold another event there, give the maître d' or head of waiters something extra (about $50) as well as any particularly good waiters (about $25). Don't give these extras to the catering director to distribute because he may not get it to the right people.

TIP: Check the amount of the gratuity that's added to the bill; it's negotiable. Also, check to see if you have been charged tax. As a nonprofit organization, you don't have to pay it.

Food as Main Event

While food is often part of a larger event, it can also be the reason for an event. Let's face it, people love to eat and giving them what they love can mean big money.

A case in point is the chili festival held in Fort Lauderdale, Florida. The event attracted 100 entrants with their beloved chili recipes, each of whom paid $50 to enter. Each entrant had a booth and cooked his or her favorite recipe.

The children's charity planning the event anticipated 5,000 attendees. They lined up major sponsors—a radio station and beer distributor—and got permission to use a city park. The charity sent out fliers and advertised the contest heavily, especially the large cash prize for the winner. Besides the $50 each entrant paid, those who attended each paid $3 at the gate. Here the food was the main attraction, and good food alone was enough to bring people out. The event raised $50,000 for the charity.

You can stage all types of food events. Pick a theme: Italian, Mexican, chocolate, seafood, garlic, area restaurant specialties. You reserve the site, rent booths out to vendors, and charge people admission to enter. Add some music and a nice setting and you are likely to make a lot of money while giving people a good time.

CHECKLIST

☐ Assess the event's market, scope, location, time, and budget. Determine what sort of food would be appropriate.

☐ Develop list of hotels/caterers. Visit each and meet with catering director to discuss possible menus, costs. (If doing your own cooking, have committee meet to discuss menus, try out recipes.)

☐ Negotiate contract.

☐ If using a caterer, determine what equipment your staff will need to rent; assign person to oversee this.

☐ A week before the event, provide guarantee; finalize two days before the event (in writing).

☐ If preparing your own food, develop shopping list; arrange for people to shop and cook.

☐ Determine what beverages will be served.

☐ Arrange for meals/snacks for staff who will set up site.

☐ Prepare and serve food.

☐ Arrange to take leftovers to a homeless shelter.

☐ Tip serving staff an additional amount if service was good and you plan to use the hotel/caterer again.

Chapter 8

Read All About It

Once you have a theme and a date, it's time to start selling your product. Word of mouth is the cheapest and, often, the most effective way to promote your event. Ask your volunteers to talk to people in the community and to recruit others. You might want to have them develop a target list that reflects a cross section of your community. Those most likely to be able to spread the word are those who come into contact with a lot of people. Among these are store owners, hairdressers, accountants, lawyers, stockbrokers, physicians, real estate agents, and anyone else with a large client base. They talk to many people every day.

Media Promotion

A prime but often overlooked avenue for advertising is tying media promotion with ticket sales. Try arranging a contest with a radio or television station or newspaper. In exchange for a specified number of on-air spots or print ads promoting the event, the charity will give a specific number of tickets away as prizes for the contest. This creates repeated, large-scale exposure for the event and helps promote outside sales. Figures 8-1 through 8-3 demonstrates how such an arrangement is finalized.

You can also buy advertising, just as any company does. Papers and radio and TV stations sometimes offer charities lower rates. Don't forget smaller weekly papers, many of which are distributed free and so have great exposure along with substantially lower ad rates. If you have a large corporate sponsor, it might be willing to buy commercial time or ad space for the charity in return for promoting the corporation's product at the same time.

When the University of Miami Burn Center held a scavenger hunt in downtown Miami, the *Miami Herald* donated $7,500 in advertising. The names of all the sponsors, including the *Herald*, were printed on the event T-shirts, on banners in the refreshment area, and at some spot along the route. The paper agreed to participate because it brought people into the downtown area and supported the burn center.

TIP: Ask companies that send out regular mailings—banks, utilities, department stores—to let you include a stuffer. You provide the actual enclosures or camera-ready copy according to the company's specifications. It's a good way to get broad publicity at very little cost.

Invitation Events

Normally, events for which invitations are sent out follow standard direct mail procedures. Good lists are the keys to success. Your carefully selected chairmen form committees, then the members provide names and addresses of all the affluent community people they know. Add to that the names of anyone who previously contributed to your cause. If possible, acquire lists from other charities and organizations (or client lists from businesses). Then merge all of these so no one gets multiple invitations.

TIP: By compiling your mailing list well in advance, you will know how many invitations you will need.

Figure 8-1. Follow-up Letter to Request Radio Station Sponsorship

Transplant Foundation of South Florida

November 13, 1990

Mr. Paul Cook
Marketing Director
WAXY-FM
1975 East Sunrise Blvd.
Ft. Lauderdale, Florida 33304

Dear Paul:

Thank you so very much for meeting with me to discuss the Peter Max Art Show to benefit the Transplant Foundation of South Florida. This show is scheduled for Friday evening January 18th, 1991 at the Design Center of The Americas (DCOTA) Dania, Florida.

As we discussed, we would like WAXY to give us 30 to 40 spots during the 10 days prior to the show. We would like WAXY also to be included in our Peter Max Art raffle which will include additional trips and items. I will also work towards getting Peter Max studios to provide some signed Grammy Posters for on air give-a-ways.

Please let me know at your earliest convenience how WAXY-FM will be involved so that I can finalize my planning.

Thank you in advance for your interest.

Sincerely,

Harry Freedman
Executive Director

HF/pdl

Figure 8-2. Proposal for Radio Station Sponsorship

December 3, 1990

Mr. Harry Freedman
HARRY FREEDMAN & ASSOC., INC.
729 N.E. 71st Street
Miami, Florida 33138

Dear Harry:

WAXY is looking forward to working with you for the Peter Max Art
opening to benefit the Transplant Foundation of South Florida on
January 18, 1991.

WAXY will promote the benefit through a new "showcase" feature
during Rick Shaw's show, afternoons between 2 and 6 p.m.   The
feature is called "Rick Shaw's Classic Showcase".   The feature
focuses on classic events, music, memorabilia etc. The idea is to
promote the event as a classic night out with a classic artist.
The show also features classic music from the 60's and 70's so it's
a nice marriage with Peter Max and the event.

Twice a day during the week of January 7th, Rick will conduct
trivia related to the era and correct callers will win the signed
grammy poster, and qualify to win the two $3,000 seriographs.
All on-air spots will mention your sponsor Chase Manhattan Bank of
South Florida.

WAXY to Provide	Value
12 On-air qualifying :60 contests	$2,500
2 Grand Prize Giveaways	200
35 :60 recorded promos	7,000
1 On-air interview with Peter Max	
Total on-air value	$9,700

Harry Freedman Associates (Thru VIA MAX)

-12 autographed 1991 Grammy Posters
- 2 Peter Max original seriographs signed and numbered ($6,000
  value)

- An interview with Peter Max (prior to January 7th) at either our
  studio or thru the phone.

Figure 8-3. Confirmation of Radio Station Sponsorship

Transplant Foundation of South Florida

December 27, 1990

Mr. Paul Cook
WAXY-FM
1975 East Sunrise Blvd.
Fort Lauderdale, Florida 33304

Dear Paul:

This letter is to request radio sponsorship by WAXY-FM for the Transplant Foundation of South Florida's Peter Max Art Show. This preview of Peter Max Rock/Pop Images will kick-off a national five city tour introducing new works of art and the 1991 Grammy Poster.
Peter Max will be attending the opening which is scheduled for Friday evening, January 18, 1991 at the Design Center of The Americas (DCOTA).

This event is a major fundraiser for the Transplant Foundation of South Florida. Our Foundation provides extensive patient services, public education and research as related to transplantation (see enclosed material). We are among the leading transplant programs in the United States with an 85% success rate for adult kidney transplants.

We would like WAXY-FM to give us (50) radio public service announcements to help promote this event.

In return for your involvement we would provide:

1. Your name and logo on 15,000 invitations to the event.
2. Recognition on all print and other media releases.
3. Be listed on all door prize tickets giving away a Peter Max seriograph, a cruise and other prizes.
4. Space to display information about WAXY-FM at the Design Center the evening of the event.
5. Thru VIA MAX 12 signed Grammy Posters for on-air give-a-ways, and 2 limited edition seriographs valued at $3,000 each for an on-air contest.
6. An advanced on-air interview with Peter Max.

1150 N.W. 14th Street • Suite 208 • Miami, Florida 33136
Telephone: (305) 545-6816 • Fax: (305) 545-6902

We are expecting over 3,000 individuals to attend this event as well as having extensive media coverage.

I have enclosed some additional information about Peter Max and the upcoming show for your review.   This would be an excellent opportunity for WAXY-FM to assist the Transplant Foundation while having the opportunity for an exciting on-air promotion which also brings attention to your radio station.

I look forward to your positive response.

Sincerely,

Marty Freedman
Executive Director

HF/pdl

Enclosures

If you have an identifiable image, use it. The Burn Center uses Snuffy, a dalmatian and the mascot for a talking fire-fighting truck used in the burn center's educational program. Fire fighting and dalmatians are a natural combination. The burn center has used Snuffy's image over the years, dressing him appropriately for each event. For a beach party, for example, he wore a Hawaiian shirt and sunglasses. For a scavenger hunt, he donned a Sherlock Holmes cape and pipe. For an auction, he wore a red bow tie and tuxedo (see figure 8-4). The burn center's lettering is fire-engine red accompanied by the dalmatian, so people came to associate the image and colors with the charity.

Besides a distinctive symbol, invitations should include:

- the name of the event
- the sponsoring organization
- time and date
- location
- purpose and theme
- committee and chairmen
- cost and to whom checks should be made out
- deadline for response
- honorees, if any
- what will be served (lunch, cocktails, etc.)
- attire
- board of directors (optional)
- return envelope and reply card

TIP: Arrange to have returns mailed to a prominent person in the community; you get better response if replies go to a well-known person instead of an impersonal company.

Along with all this information, the invitation should be attractive and eye-catching. Examples are portrayed in figures 8-5 through 8-8.

Don't forget to have save-the-date cards printed to be sent out well in advance of the event and at least several weeks before the invitations. Figure 8-9 shows three examples of these.

Figure 8-4. University of Miami Burn Center Invitation Using Snuffy

Figure 8-5. Invitation Package for 1989 Grand Prix Gala

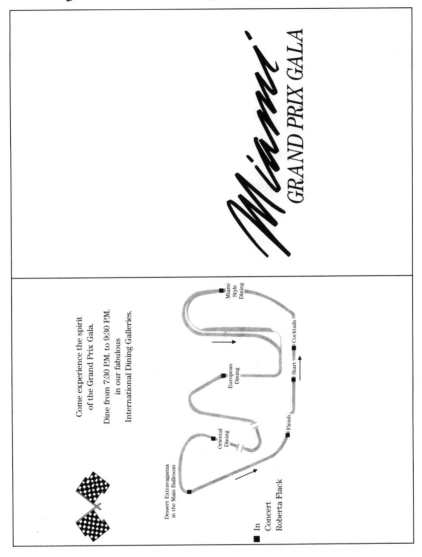

You are cordially invited
to attend the

1989 GRAND PRIX GALA

at the

Omni International Hotel
Ballroom Level

Friday, March 3, 1989

7:30 P.M. Dining Galleries
10:00 P.M. Dessert Extravaganza
followed by

Roberta Flack in Concert

Proceeds will benefit
UM JM Burn Center
Mailman Child Development Center
The Learning Experience School

Black Tie

Red, White or Black Attire Suggested

1989 GRAND PRIX GALA

■ Honorary Chairpersons
Tony and Joyce Burns

■ Chairperson
Eleanor Kroon

■ Executive Chairpersons
Rafael and Lourdes Sanchez

■ Co-Chairpersons
Kathy Simkins   Blanca Suarez   Rosario Vadia

■ Steering Committee
Marta Almeyra
Dorothy Ash
Carole Christoff
Harriet Dash
Remedios Diaz-Oliver
Barry Freedman

Dr. Jeffrey Hammond
Monica Heller
Yolanda E. Hospital
Jeffrey Kroon Werner
Martha Modrecin
Georgina Montesdeoca
Maria Rosa Lopez Mimo

■ Honorary Committee
Mrs. Bernard Abel
Mr. and Mrs. Emilio Alonso-Mendoza
Mrs. Bette Arango
Mr. Raul Arango
Mr. and Mrs. Ricardo Arregui
Mr. and Mrs. Stephen N. Ashman
Mr. Felix Barash
Mr. and Mrs. Jose Barea
Mr. and Mrs. Wendell Beard
Mr. and Mrs. Joaquin Blaya
Mrs. Nora Bulnes
Mr. and Mrs. Alvaro M. Cabrera
Mr. and Mrs. Randy Coleman
Mr. Walter Crewson
Mr. and Mrs. Luis Del Pino
Mr. and Mrs. Alan Dalton

Mr. and Mrs. George Feldenkreis
Mr. and Mrs. Emerson Fittipaldi
Mr. and Mrs. Diego Gamez
Dr. and Mrs. Jeffrey Hammond
Mr. and Mrs. Abel Holtz
Daniel Holtz
Mr. and Mrs. F. Edwin Jackman
Ms. Karen Keenan
Mr. and Mrs. Russell Kleiser
Mrs. Mary LeBrun
Mr. and Mrs. Robert W. Lesher
Mr. and Mrs. German Leiva
Dr. Anita Licistein
Mr. and Mrs. Juan Lopez
Mr. and Mrs. Robert Marlin

Jeanin Roberts
Ana Soler
Maria Vadia
Dr. C. Cullen Ward
Ruth A. Wasserthal-Gold
Connie Wollman

Mr. and Mrs. Fausto Marquez
Mr. Ron Mashburn
Mr. and Mrs. Carlos Migoya
Mr. and Mrs. Leonard Miller
Mr. and Mrs. Benjamin Nameth
Mr. Steven Neckman
Dr. and Mrs. Emilio Pacheco
Mr. Robert Pascal
Mr. Carlos Plana
Dr. and Mrs. Willie Robinson
Mr. Fausto Sanchez
Mr. and Mrs. Eduardo Sardiña
Mr. and Mrs. Rob Sanchez
Mr. Lee Brian Schrager
Mr. Jose Valdés-Fauli
Dr. and Mrs. C. Cullen Ward
Mr. and Mrs. Sherwood Weiser

■ Corporate Sponsors
BELLSOUTH MOBILITY
MARTINI & ROSSI

NISSAN MOTOR CORPORATION
PENRODS BEACH CLUB

Partial list

1989 GRAND PRIX GALA

Omni International Hotel
Friday, March 3, 1989

Please reserve the following:

_____ Individual seat(s) at $150 each

_____ Benefactor seat(s) at $250 each

_____ Benefactor table(s) at $2,500 each (10 seats)

_____ Corporate table(s) at $3,500 each (10 seats)
(Includes two Grand Prix VIP Club memberships)

A check in the amount of $_____ , made payable
to the Grand Prix Gala, is enclosed.*

I cannot attend, but enclosed is my donation of $_____

Name _____

Address _____

City/State/Zip _____

*For tax purposes deduct $60 from the price of each seat purchased. Contributions will be acknowledged
from UM School of Medicine.

The following persons will be my guests:

_____   _____

_____   _____

_____   _____

_____   _____

Please seat me with:

_____   _____

_____   _____

_____   _____

_____   _____

PLACE
STAMP
HERE

Miami

GRAND PRIX GALA

Mrs. Eleanor Kosow, Chairperson
University of Miami
School of Medicine
1500 N.W. 12th Avenue, Suite 1021
Miami, Florida 33136

Figure 8-6. Invitation to Peter Max Exhibition

"The Grammys, 1991", © Peter Max, 1990

Sally Ann and Howard Rosenbaum
cordially invite you to a private
preview of a major exhibition of
works by internationally acclaimed artist

PETER MAX

to benefit the
TRANSPLANT FOUNDATION OF SOUTH FLORIDA

CHAMPAGNE RECEPTION
FRIDAY, JANUARY 18, 1991
7:00-9:00 pm
Special Guest: Peter Max

ROSENBAUM GALLERY
Design Center of the Americas (DCOTA)
1855 Griffin Road, Suite B280
Dania, Florida

105.9 WAXY FM

RSVP
923-6638

 CHASE

Figure 8-7. Invitation to Kick-off Party for 1988 Grand Prix Gala

Figure 8-8. Invitation and Response Card for 1991 Hooters Superweek Golf Classic

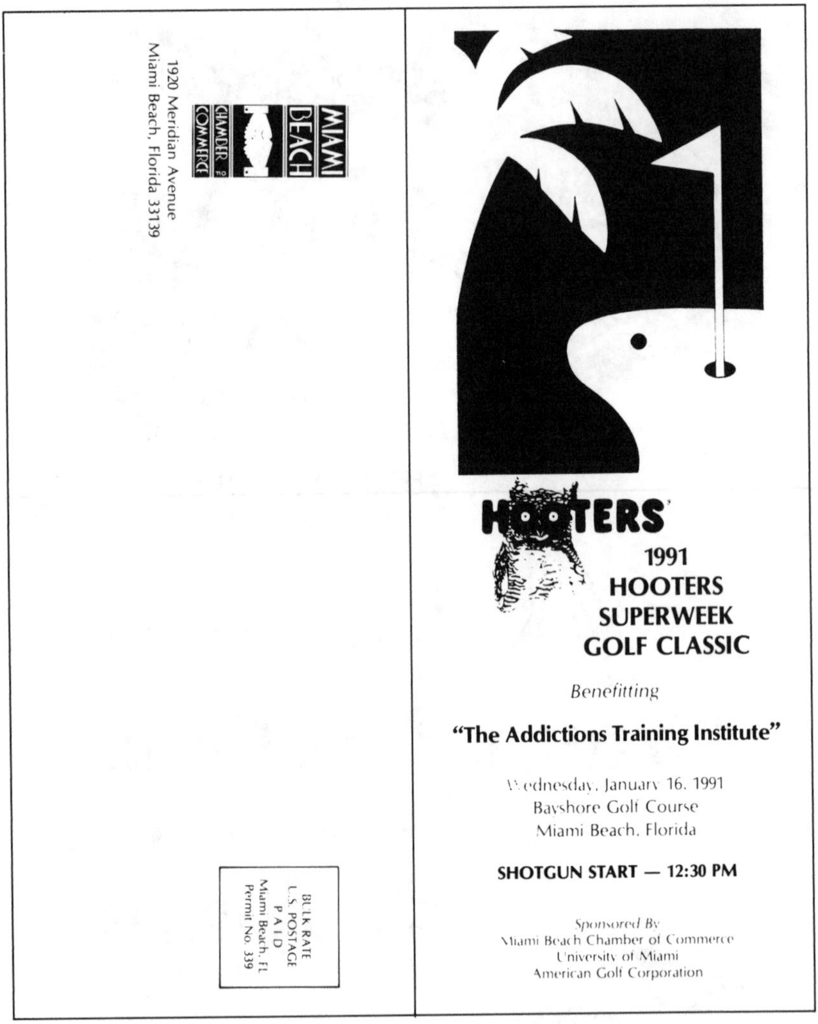

MIAMI BEACH CHAMBER OF COMMERCE
1920 Meridian Avenue
Miami Beach, Florida 33139

BULK RATE
U.S. POSTAGE
PAID
Miami Beach, FL
Permit No. 339

HOOTERS
1991
HOOTERS
SUPERWEEK
GOLF CLASSIC

Benefitting

"The Addictions Training Institute"

Wednesday, January 16, 1991
Bayshore Golf Course
Miami Beach, Florida

SHOTGUN START — 12:30 PM

Sponsored By
Miami Beach Chamber of Commerce
University of Miami
American Golf Corporation

Dear Friend

This letter is to request your participation in the Third Annual Superweek Golf Tournament hosted by the Miami Beach Chamber of Commerce and to benefit the Addictions Training Institute

One in every ten persons is addicted to drugs and alcohol. Millions of others suffer from addictive behaviors. Consequently, there is an acute need for trained professionals who can provide competent guidance and counseling to individuals and their families

The Addictions Training Institute, formerly the Chemical Dependency Training Institute, is the only internationally recognized program in South Florida to train individuals to become Certified Addiction Professionals. This program, affiliated with the University of Miami's School of Continuing Studies is our communities's best hope in the battle against drugs and alcohol abuse, and other addictive behaviors

You can make a difference by attending the Golf Tournament or becoming a hole or cart sponsor for this event. Your financial support will be used to provide important scholarship money to train Addiction Counselors

Compared to governmental spending of millions on the 'War On Drugs' and with the personal costs we all pay as the result of crime and disease related to addiction, your support of our scholarship program is a great investment in a better community!"

Please send your check or commitment today!

Tom Sledd, C.A.P.
President
The Addiction Training Institute

MIAMI BEACH CHAMBER 9 COMMERCE

Dear Friends

The **Miami Beach Chamber of Commerce and The University of Miami** are proud to host the celebrity studded 1991 **"Superweek Golf Classic"** benefitting the Addictions Training Institute. We are excited to share this event with this year's major corporate sponsor HOOTERS

This Golf Tournament and Barbecue Dinner will help raise important scholarship money for the training of addiction counselors

For more information regarding how your business can participate and take advantage of this 'Superweek' promotional opportunity, contact the Miami Beach Chamber of Commerce at 672-1270

This year's event, during Super Bowl XXV week, promises to be the most memorable. Your sponsorship of one of the packages described in this brochure would be a major contribution to this year's success

We look forward to sharing this 'Super Day' with you

A. Anthony Noboa, Chairman of the Board
Miami Beach Chamber of Commerce

Mike Burris, Chairman
1991 Superweek Golf Classic

HALL OF FAME
$850.00

- Hole Sponsor (Choice of hole & tee)
- Cart Sponsor (sign)
- Special acknowledgement in Tournament program and in all promotional publications
- Four (4) complimentary players
- Cocktail Reception and Dinner for four

ALL PRO
$50.00

- Corporate or individual sign on golf cart
- Attendance at tournament, including Cocktail Reception & Dinner for one

FAN CLUB
$25.00

- Attendance at tournament, including Cocktail and Dinner for one

SUPERSTAR'S CLUB
$350.00

- Hole Sponsor (Choice of hole)
- Cart Sponsor (sign)
- Special acknowledgement in Tournament program and in the Miami Beach Chamber Newsletter
- Two (2) complimentary players
- Cocktail Reception and Dinner for two

PLAYER SPONSORSHIP
$100.00
(play or sponsor a celebrity)

- Green and Cart fees
- Cocktail Reception & Dinner for one
- Tournament souvenirs

Special Hole-in-One Prize:

**1985
Ferrari Testarrosa
From Shelton Ferrari
17th Hole**

TOURNAMENT FORMAT

A "Captain's Choice Scramble" Event. All
players drive from tee and select the best shot.
The same procedure is used on all shots,
including putts. Prizes will be awarded in both
net and gross categories. The registration for
the Tournament is limited to the first 144
players. So get your reservation in now!

TOURNAMENT DAY
WEDNESDAY, JANUARY 16, 1991
SHOTGUN START   12:30 PM
AT
BAYSHORE GOLF COURSE
2301 ALTON ROAD
MIAMI BEACH, FLORIDA

PRE-TOURNAMENT ACTIVITIES

DRIVING RANGE OPEN 10:30 AM 12:00 PM
CHIP AND PUTT CONTESTS
LUNCH

AWARD CEREMONY,
ENTERTAINMENT & DINNER
IMMEDIATELY FOLLOWING TOURNAMENT

TOURNAMENT FEATURES
Captain's Choice Scramble
Limited to 36 foursomes
Lunch and Dinner
Refreshment Carts on the Course
Souvenir Photos
Hole-in-1 prize: 1985 Ferrary Testarrosa
from Shelton Ferrari
Contest: Longest Drive, Closest-to-pin
& others

For more information please call
672-1270 or 532-3350

AMERICAN GOLF CORPORATION

1991 HOOTERS SUPERWEEK GOLF CLASSIC

NAME _____ DAY PHONE _____ ZIP _____
PREFERRED MAILING ADDRESS _____ CITY _____ ZIP _____

My foursome includes: (Open foursome will be filled)

NAME _____ DAY PHONE _____ ZIP _____
NAME _____ DAY PHONE _____ ZIP _____
NAME _____ DAY PHONE _____ ZIP _____

SPONSORSHIPS

Hall of Fame ($850.00) _____   Superstar's Club ($350.00) _____
Player or Sponsorship ($100.00) _____   All pro ($50.00) _____
Fan Club ($25.00) _____

Please have my sign and acknowledgements read: _____

Make checks payable to:
SUPERWEEK GOLF CLASSIC

Detach and return to:
Miami Beach Chamber of Commerce
1920 Meridian Avenue
Miami Beach, Florida 33139

Figure 8-9. Three Sample Save-the-Date Cards

THERE'S NO BUSINESS LIKE SHOW BUSINESS: STAGE 2

STARRING PHYLLIS DILLER

SAVE THE DATE!

JOIN CELEBRITY GUEST
PHYLLIS DILLER FOR
"THERE'S NO BUSINESS LIKE SHOW
BUSINESS."

MONDAY, MARCH 11, 1991
AT THE GREAT HALL,
BOCA RATON RESORT AND CLUB.

SAVE THIS DATE FOR AN ELEGANT
EVENING OF ENTERTAINMENT,
DINING AND DANCING TO BENEFIT
THE TRANSPLANT FOUNDATION
OF SOUTH FLORIDA.

FOR FURTHER INFORMATION,
CONTACT:
　　　　HARRY FREEDMAN
　　　　(305) 545-6816

BACK TO BACK BASHES

to benefit the University of Miami/Jackson Memorial Burn Center

**South Florida's
Biggest
Beach Bash**
Sunday
February 4, 1990
9:00 a.m. to 5:00 p.m.

**PENROD'S
AT THE BEACH**

Volleyball Tournaments
Beach Girl/Beach Guy Contest
Food and Celebrity Entertainment

**The Great
Snuffy Hunt**
Saturday
February 10, 1990
7:30 p.m. to midnight
Throughout Downtown Miami

Clues, Prizes
and Surprises

Non-Profit
U.S. Postage
P A I D
Permit No. 438
Miami, Florida

SAVE THE DATE!

NATIONAL PARKINSON FOUNDATION

SAVE THE DATE:
SUNDAY, MARCH 2, 1986, 5:30 P.M.
OMNI INTERNATIONAL HOTEL

CARLOS J. ARBOLEYA

WILL RECEIVE THE NATIONAL PARKINSON FOUNDATION'S
1986 HUMANITARIAN AWARD AT THE ANNUAL

GALA FOR HOPE

WITH PERFORMANCES BY
BOB HOPE, DICK CLARK, PETER ALLEN,
PHYLLIS DILLER, DOLORES HOPE

FOR INFORMATION, CALL 547-6666

FORMAL INVITATION TO FOLLOW

*P.S. Dolores and I are looking forward
to being with you March 2nd.*

Bob Hope, Chairman
Board of Governors

NON-PRO-ORG.
U.S. POSTAGE
PAID
MIAMI, FLORIDA
PERMIT NO. 723

Ordering Invitations

The first thing you need to determine is the number of invitations you need (the number on your mailing list plus 25 percent for publicity, extras to hand out, and a back-up supply). How many pieces will the invitation be (outside envelope, inside envelope, invitation, reply card, return envelope, personal note card)?

You'll need a graphic artist to design an appealing invitation. Make sure he understands postal regulations regarding size and weight. Discuss with the artist how many colors of ink and the kinds of paper you would like used. How expensive do you want it to look? You don't want it to look as lavish as those for weddings or bar mitzvahs or it will appear you have spent too much money. (The exception to this rule is when the cost of the invitations is totally underwritten.) With design in hand, you're ready to have your invitation printed.

Ask around for reputable printers and try to get at least three bids. (See the sample bid in figure 8-10.) Always check references, too, making sure to ask each person whether the printer not only delivered good quality work but did so on time. Find out if the printer will provide the invitation in pieces or will fold it and put it together for you. (If you have to assemble them, you'll need more people to fold, assemble, and stuff.)

TIP: Ask to receive the envelopes in advance in order to begin addressing them.

Once you get the artwork for the invitation, proofread it carefully to make sure all the information is correct. Double-check the date, time, and place, and spelling of committee members' and sponsors' names. If possible, have three or four people proofread it. (This may sound silly, but all too often invitations that have not been checked go out lacking vital information—such as the time or date—or containing wrong information.)

Time Frame

Remember that all of this has to be done fairly well in advance of the event. Invitations should be mailed four to six weeks before

Figure 8-10. Sample Printer's Bid

McFarland & Drier, Inc.

3750 Coral Way, Miami, FL 33145   Advertising   (305) 858 6757

PRODUCTION ESTIMATE OF COSTS ON JOB #   FAL-1057   DATE: 9/4/86

CLIENT: Falls

DESCRIPTION: Invitation/Reply Card/2-envelopes & note card

(This is an ESTIMATE only. Changes and unanticipated problems
increase costs and require a revised estimate.)

Layout/Design		COLLATERAL SPECIFICATIONS
Mechanical		Quantity: 3M/5M
Mechanical Supervision		Size 7 x 28½ Inv. 7 x 4-3/4
		Flat: A-7 Env. #4 baronia Folded:
Photography		Stock: card & env. 100# gloss text-inv.
Photo Supervision		24# white wove-all env.
		80# uncoated cover - cards
Model (s)		
Film & Processing and Prints		
Retouching		No. of Pages:
Illustration		Colors: 1/1 Black or 2/1 metallic silver & black-Inv. 1/0 Black all other material
Conversion Prints		No. Separations/Halftones: screen all pieces
Typography	300	
Photostats	25	Binding: flap
Engraving/Veloxes		
Separations		

		Printing Services	Fine Arts	Dependable Printing	
Printing Quotes (Incl. % contingency)	3M	2,234	1,650	2,050	Additional Remarks:
	5M	3,067	2,330	2,635	*Additional gross cost for silver: 3M=$206
Sub-total	3M		1,975		5M=$235
	5M		2,655		
Agency Commission					Client Approval
					Title
Grand Total (Shipping cost & Fla. State Sales Tax additional)	3M		1,975 +806 = $8181		Date
	5M		2,655 +235 = $2890		

the date. Add to that a minimum of two weeks to have the invitations designed and about three weeks to get them printed. And allow yourself at least a week to address and mail the invitations. That means you need to start working on this about three months before your event. If possible, add an extra month to allow for missed deadlines.

Getting Them Out

Set up a schedule for volunteers to address invitations. (If you have access to one, a computer will make this job much easier.) Keep a master mailing list and make a copy from which the volunteers work. The best way to maintain control of this is to have volunteers come to a central location to work. As each invitation is addressed, a check mark is placed next to the name.

Whenever possible, committee members should add personal notes to those people they know. These are then inserted with the invitations.

If you plan to mail the invitations at bulk rate (you can do this for as few as 500 invitations, but you probably won't save much if you mail fewer than 1,000 pieces), you'll need to sort invitations into boxes according to zip code. You can have a mailing house do this for you, but you'll incur an additional expense. While it takes extra time, it can save money since the bulk rate is about half that of first class.

Once the invitations are all addressed, the person in charge should personally take them to the post office. That way, you are sure they got mailed and are not sitting on someone's kitchen table. If you can't get people to come to a central location to address the envelopes (many people like to work at home), ask that they return the completed invitations to the office so you can still mail them yourself.

Follow-Up Calls

Once the invitations are out, start working the phones. Using the same master list, assign portions to each of the committee people. (All mailing lists should have phone numbers on them for just these sorts of follow-ups.)

TIP: Following up the invitations with phone calls significantly boosts attendance.

Callers should have a script that includes a key reason for someone to attend: "I'm Jane Jones, a volunteer with the XYZ Charity. Mrs. Smith asked me to follow up on the invitation she sent you to our event. She was sure that you would like to join her that evening. Can I put you down for two seats?" (A sample script is shown in figure 8-11.)

For a corporation, try something like: "I know your corporation will want to join our other corporate sponsors, which include FGH Inc. and XYZ Corp."

It's typical of people to wait to the last minute. Keep at it. Make a second round of calls, if necessary. Have some volunteers call businesspeople at their offices during the day. Have others make calls to people at home in the evening.

Promotion

The next step is to get the word out to the general public. Along with ticket sales, promotion is one of the most important aspects of planning an event. It's vital to put one very responsible person in charge of this. If you don't have a person you can trust to handle it properly, consider hiring a publicist or public relations firm (make sure this is included in your budget).

Your most effective means of getting the word out is the news media. Carefully prepare a media list and include all radio and television stations and newspapers (weeklies, college, schools, in-house newsletters, local magazines). Check with your local chamber of commerce and consult the Yellow Pages to make sure your list is comprehensive. Call each one on the list and find out who your release should be addressed to (the specific department and, if

Figure 8-11. Sample Telephone Script to Follow Up Invitation

GALA FOR HOPE
PHONE CAMPAIGN

Suggested Script

My name is _____ and I am a ___Friend___ of the National
                                   Board Member

Parkinson Foundation, donating my time for this special telephone drive for
our annual Bob Hope Benefit Concert and Dinner.

I am sure you have already received the invitation to this event.
This year we must increase private support so that we can continue our
important research, diagnostic and service programs.

For this year's benefit, many friends have purchased $250 tickets
which entitle them to excellent seats at our show and inclusion in our
dinner with the stars following the concert. We were sure we could
count on your support.

If "Yes":

  1. Review name, address and phone numbers.

  2. Do you still have our return envelope, or should I send you another.

  3. Special and warm "Thank You" for support.

If "No":

  1. Could we interest you in other price tickets: $100 with cocktail
     party and $50 good seats concert only.

If "Absolutely No":

  1. Be positive as possible Close with hope that donation or future
     gift be considered.

possible, the person who would handle it) and what the deadlines are. Get a FAX number, too.

Prepare a concise news release and direct it to the person at each area radio and television station who handles public service announcements (PSAs)—15-, 30-, or 60-second items usually read by an announcer. These must be short and to the point. Just give the basics. Figure 8-12 shows a news release and figure 8-13 is a public service announcement.

Remember that your PSA will compete against many others for air time so the more unusual yours is, the more likely it is to be used. One way to do this is to have celebrities tape them for you. If you know a star will be appearing in town, call in advance to see if he or she will be willing to tape your PSA. These are usually arranged through the personal manager or publicist.

TIP: If the celebrity appears on one television network, don't offer that PSA to a competing station. Chances are, the competition won't use it.

The University of Miami Burn Center used this strategy successfully in a series of fire safety messages. Bill Harris, who hosts Showtime's "At the Movies," willingly taped a message and arranged to have Howie Mandell do the same when he appeared on the show. Other stars who were happy to tape these messages were Bob Hope, Estelle Getty ("Golden Girls") and Phyllis Diller.

Newspapers have community calendars and weekend entertainment guides. Don't assume the departments swap releases—each gets hundreds a day. Send one to each possible outlet. Send releases to daily newspapers two to three weeks in advance of the event. For monthly magazines, the lead time is six to eight weeks. For convention calendars, send information as soon as you get it because they are often printed far in advance (quarterly or semiannually).

For radio and television promotion, arrange for your PSA three to four weeks before the event. Send a news release to the appropriate person, including a cover letter. Sometimes you can tie into public service themes the stations run. Some stations sponsor year-long promotions, focusing on such things as children's issues

Figure 8-12. News Release for 1989 Grand Prix Gala

 NEWS RELEASE

DATE **FOR IMMEDIATE PRESS RELEASE PLEASE!!**   Harry A. Freedman   CONTACT

PLANS FOR GRAND PRIX GALA ANNOUNCED

The 1989 Grand Prix Gala will be held on Friday evening, March 3, 1989 at the Omni International Hotel. The Grand Prix Gala has become recognized as one of the premiere national events of the Miami social season. Over one thousand people are expected to attend this charity event which kicks off the Grand Prix race weekend, and will raise funds for the UM/JM Burn Center, the Mailman Center for Child Development, and the Learning School Experience.

The 1989 Gala should be the most spectacular and unusual event held in the history of the Miami Grand Prix. Guests will arrive on the Ballroom Level at the Omni International Hotel and given a map which will resemble the Grand Prix race track, but in fact, will "steer" guests to three international dining galleries. The dining galleries will have food from the Orient, Europe, and Miami style food (to include Latin, Jewish, American, etcetera). Between 7:30 and 9:30 p.m. guests can sample international cuisine and listen to entertainment reflecting the countries represented.

At 10:00 p.m. guests will move into the Main Ballroom for a dessert extravaganza, followed by ROBERTA FLACK in concert. "We are quite thrilled to have the extraordinary talent of ROBERTA FLACK to entertain at this year's Gala event", said

P.O. Box 016310, Miami, Florida 33101   (305) 547-6256

Mr. & Mrs. Rafael Sanchez, Executive Chairpersons of the event.

ROBERTA FLACK released her first album in 1968 with Atlantic Records, and received her first Grammy Award in March of 1973 for the song "First Time Ever I Saw Your Face". This song was also voted record of the year, and was followed by the album "Killing Me Softly With His Song", which was a certified gold record within two weeks after its release. In 1974 "Killing Me Softly" was the Grammy Record of the year. ROBERTA FLACK has had continued success as a Rhythm and Blues singer, and most recently released "Oasis" which is breaking chart records. The new album has songs by many well-known composers such as Ashford & Simpson, David Sanborn, Marvin Hamlisch, Quincy Jones, with several songs written by ROBERTA FLACK herself.

Major sponsors for the Grand Prix Gala include BellSouth Mobility, Nissan Motor Corporaton, and Martini & Rossi. Tickets for the Gala are available by contacting the University of Miami School of Medicine, Development Office, (305) 547-6256, at $150 Patron and $250 Benefactor (preferred seating). Packages are available which include seats at the Gala and Grand Prix Race VIP Club memberships.

Early reservations are suggested as the Grand Prix Gala is sure to be a sell-out.

Interviews with ROBERTA FLACK can be set up IN ADVANCE ONLY by contacting Harry A. Freedman, (305) 547-6256.

Figure 8-13. Public Service Announcement Script for "Gala for Hope"

NATIONAL PARKINSON FOUNDATION, INC.

- BOB HOPE PARKINSON RESEARCH CENTER
- PARKINSON DIAGNOSTIC REHABILITATION TREATMENT AND CARE INSTITUTE

Bob Hope
National Chairman

```
THIS IS BOB - ON THE ROAD - HOPE, IN MIAMI

SUNDAY, FEBRUARY 24 FOR MY 25TH "GALA FOR HOPE"

FOR THE NATIONAL PARKINSON FOUNDATION -- THE

GREATEST SHOW EVER IN SOUTH FLORIDA.  COME

TO THE KNIGHT CENTER, FEBRUARY 24, AND

CELEBRATE WITH DICK CLARK, PETER ALLEN, RAPHAEL,

RIO BY NIGHT, PHYLLIS DILLER, AL MARTINO, JOEY

BISHOP, SID CAESAR AND MANY OTHERS.  HELP THE

PARKINSON FOUNDATION AND HAVE AN EVENING WITH

THE STARS.  FOR TICKETS CALL 547-6666.
```

National Parkinson Institute • 1501 N.W. 9th Ave. Bob Hope Road • Miami, Florida 33136 • Phone (305) 547-6666
New York Office • 122 East 42nd Street • New York, N.Y. 10017 • Phone (212) 374-1741
Associated with University of Miami School of Medicine
Toll Free 1-800-327-4545 • Florida Toll Free 1-800-433-7022

or antidrug campaigns. If your group fits into that category, you might be able to tie in with the station's campaign. If you have corporate sponsors, check to see if they will pay (or help pay) for advertising. Figure 8-14 shows a sample newspaper ad paid for by sponsors.

TIP: Ask committee members if they know people who work in the media, and try to work through them.

Besides PSAs, there is news coverage. Start by distributing press kits. They contain a cover letter, news release, fact sheet, organization information, sponsor list, poster, and photos (if available and of good quality).

In most cases, no matter how important you think your event is, most of the news media won't think it's newsworthy. So how do you get coverage? Find an angle that will interest an editor. Be creative.

When the South Florida Transplant Foundation planned a golf tournament in Naples, Florida, the executive director contacted an editor of the local paper's feature department with an idea for a health story about a committee member whose life was saved through the organization's work. That was a good way to lead into a story about the charity and its tournament. This way, the group got publicity first in the form of a story, then in the paper's community calendar, and again in its monthly golf publication. Had that not worked, the group might have approached a medical editor about the cost of dialysis, how commonplace kidney transplants are becoming, and how they save money for insurance companies and patients.

Time Frame

Three to four weeks before the event, send the press release, mentioning the story angle briefly. Follow it up with a call, quickly restating the story angle. Make sure you already have the name and phone number of the person to be interviewed. You might follow

Figure 8-14. Sample Sponsor-Paid Newspaper Ad

LITE ROCK.LESS TALK.™

and the UM/JM Burn Center present

SOUTH FLORIDA'S
BIGGEST BEACH BASH
SUNDAY, FEBRUARY 4, 1990

at

- Volleyball Tournament
- Beach Girl/Beach Guy Contest
- Cash and other prizes

Call for information and
entry forms **(305) 547-6256**

In Concert at 4 P.M.
Gary Puckett & The Union Gap

SPONSORED BY
Publix Supermarkets   Agree Shampoo and Conditioner
The Flyer   Scandinavian Health Spas   Diet Pepsi
American Airlines   Love 94 FM   Penrod's
Irene Marie Modeling and Talent Agency

up in a few days to make sure that the reporter was able to make contact with the interviewee. And, on the chance the paper will want to cover it, send a FAX reminder the day of the event.

Support Publicity

Take advantage of any place that will let you post a notice of your event. A few examples: billboards, the backs of grocery store receipts, on grocery sacks and milk cartons, motel marquees; leave pamphlets in convenience stores, library and store bulletin boards, at visitors centers, on table tents in restaurants.

Publicity Stunts

Use these judiciously. They should be offbeat, but not crazy or offensive. Using local personalities (radio DJs, news anchors, etc.) can generate advance publicity. For a chili cook-off, for instance, hand out free chili samples at supermarkets the week before the event.

Pre-Events

Often it's hard enough to pull off the event without doing another one first. However, it can make a huge difference. A case in point: Through reading local newspapers, planners of the Miami Grand Prix knew Joan Rivers would be in Hollywood, Florida, to tape segments of the television game show, "Hollywood Squares." The Miami Grand Prix had committed part of the funds it raised that year to the University of Miami's Clinical AIDS Research Program. This was in 1987, when raising funds for AIDS was more difficult.

The group decided to contact Joan Rivers, who had previously helped raise money for AIDS programs, to see if she'd be willing to attend a preview party to promote the event. She agreed. The invitations were emblazoned with "CAN WE TALK?" (Joan Rivers's tag line), and "Meet Joan Rivers at preview event for Miami Grand Prix" (see figure 8-7). The cocktail party was held at the Grand Bay Hotel, which donated the space and food. Prior to the party, Rivers mentioned on "Hollywood Squares" and in several local television interviews that she would be at the event. While the party normally attracted 100 to 150 people, even with race-car celebrities in attendance, some 500 people came to this one, which helped to sell three-quarters of the tickets for the Grand Prix gala held a month later.

Talk Shows

Other means to promote your cause and events are through careful positioning of interesting guests and celebrities on talk shows. In most communities, radio and television stations have public service shows and talk shows on which you can arrange to appear or have someone else appear on your behalf. It's important for the person who is going to represent your cause to know that he or she must talk about the event and the group itself.

In 1990, Make-A-Wish Foundation was responsible for the Miami kickoff of artist Peter Max's "Images of an Era," a touring show of his works (see figure 8-6). Max agreed to have the first opening as a benefit for the charity, which grants wishes to children with life-threatening illnesses. Several television stations agreed to conduct live interviews during their 5 P.M. newscasts, which would be just two hours before Max's show opened.

Earlier in the day, Make-A-Wish officials prepared Max by telling him what the charity was and what the money raised would go to. They also provided him with cue cards listing the basics—what the charity is, what it does, time and place of the show.

The broadcast capped a month-long media blitz. Some 3,500 people showed up that evening at the Design Center of the Americas, raising substantial funds for the charity and prompting a major contribution from the very pleased owner of Rosenbaum Fine Art, which presented the show.

CHECKLIST

- ☐ Once you've decided upon an event, organize your sales force.
- ☐ Prepare a mailing list so you'll know how many invitations to order.
- ☐ Equip committee members with information packets, posters, and sales pitches.
- ☐ Arrange for tie-in to media promotions, if possible.
- ☐ Buy advertising.
- ☐ Have invitations designed.
- ☐ Get bids from printers and check references.
- ☐ Order invitations, arranging to have envelopes delivered first.
- ☐ Proofread invitation carefully.
- ☐ Have volunteers address invitations, including personal notes to those people they know.
- ☐ Event coordinator should collect all invitations and mail them.
- ☐ Have sales staff follow up mailing with phone calls to those who have not yet responded.
- ☐ Compile media list; send press kit.
- ☐ Arrange for public service announcements.
- ☐ Approach editors with ideas for pre-event stories.
- ☐ Arrange for additional publicity—posters, notices in utility bill mailings and on grocery receipts.
- ☐ Hold pre-event party (optional).
- ☐ Approach talk shows with timely idea for a show relating to your event.

Chapter 9

The Final Countdown

After you have survived the months or perhaps a year of planning, dealing with personalities, and trying to attend to the sea of details, the event looms near. For the ultraorganized, little remains to be done. However, in most cases, particularly at a seated event, staff members usually work right up to the wire.

At some point you have to say, "This is all I can do and this is how it will be." Say this before you stay up the whole night before; you will need to be rested for the big day. If you have been following faithfully the instructions in this book, you now have a nice, fat loose-leaf notebook. You've used the checklists to make sure everything has been covered. Now is the time to recheck. Go through each chapter checklist again; having done that, you can be fairly well assured that nothing has been forgotten.

The day before the event, check with your support staff to make sure they will be at the site early the next day. Check with all vendors to make sure they plan to show up on time. Get the phone numbers at which they can be reached outside of business hours. Check with each committee chairman to make sure you know how to reach him or her if that person won't be at the usual number.

213

Make sure the chairmen have spoken with everyone on their lists: the decorator, band, florist, etc.

TIP: Arrange for a couple of people (family members, trusted friends, or assistants) to be with you on the day of the event to deal with unexpected problems that arise. You can dispatch them to put out the smaller fires while you handle the larger tasks.

No matter what the event, there are some items you almost always need and which, invariably, are never around unless you've had the foresight to bring them yourself. Just like when you're getting ready to go to the hospital to have a baby, pack everything up in advance.

Here's what you should bring with you:

Administrative

Contact list with home and work telephone numbers
Loose-leaf notebook with all contracts, contacts, etc.
Payment for entertainer

Audio/visual

Black electrical tape/silver reflective tape
Audio/video cassettes
Extension cords
Three-prong converter
Flashlights
Needle and thread
Safety pins
Walkie-talkies (or mobile phones or beepers)

Paper Products and Related Items

Facial tissues
Toilet tissue

Paper towels
Soap
Trash bags
Paper
Scissors
Signs
Staple gun
Masking and transparent tapes
Felt-tip waterproof markers (various sizes)

First-Aid Kit

Bandages
Adhesive tape
Stretch and gauze bandages
Scissors/knife
Tweezers
Aspirin
Antacids
Alcohol and/or peroxide
Sunscreen
Insect repellent

Staff Food

Coffee
Cold drinks
Ice/ice chest
Munchies

Pack everything up the day before the event, including the clothes you plan to wear. Then, on the day itself, all you have to do is pick everything up and head out the door. If the event is in a hotel, arrange to check in a day or two in advance so you can unpack, familiarize yourself with the place, and let everyone know where to reach you. Let the front desk know that you will be receiving a number of calls and tell them where you will be. If you have a beeper, leave that number with them.

With all those things attended to, get a good night's sleep.

Registration

Registration and the work of the committee in charge of it starts long before the day of the event. One person—the chairman, secretary, or volunteer—should be in charge of keeping track of who is coming.

A system needs to be set up. It can be a computerized list or something as simple as a shoebox with alphabetized index cards inside. For each person attending a dinner, for example, the entry should list who the person wishes to sit with and his or her food preferences. If you use a computer, have someone keep a running alphabetical list of who plans to attend. Every name should have a table number listed beside it. You can also make a list with the number of tables you plan and eight spaces for each table. Fill in the names of those who will sit at each table. You can indicate whether they have paid on this same list as well.

While the actual registration is done by staff or volunteers, the seating plan is set by the chairman and a few others behind the scenes. First, those involved should walk through the room and decide how the tables will be set up. Or, in the case of an outdoor crafts show, someone must decide the lineup of vendors the same way.

Registration itself can set the tone for the event because it's the first impression your group will make on those attending. If they have to wait in long lines, are treated rudely, or encounter problems, guests may be turned off before they get in the door. To prevent such problems, place only your brightest, most courteous and flexible people at the registration tables.

Registration is usually set up about three hours before the event. If you have to feed workers, do that first, then give them a chance to get dressed. Make sure everyone on the registration staff knows how to dress for the event—generally the same as those who attend the event.

Even if your ballroom is not ready, your registration tables should be. They should be the first things that are functioning since they are the first places your guests will stop. There should be enough large (eight-foot-long) tables to allow people to sprawl out a bit. Use long tables, covered attractively and with easy-to-spot signs posted above them.

TIP: Don't put the signs on the tables themselves because they will be hidden as people gather. Make sure additional signs clearly point the way from the parking lot to the tables.

Make sure there are enough lights and electrical outlets. Use a few tables, dividing them up alphabetically, each table handling a third or a fourth of the letters. Keep another table as a troubleshooting area and one for VIPs. Place three or four chairs behind each table for registration personnel, although they will generally wind up standing as guests file by. It's always better to have too many registration workers than too few. Use your judgment: for a gathering of 100 people, you might need only one registration worker per table; for 500 people you would probably need four workers per table. If you are using computers, make sure they are all hooked up, functioning, and in a secure area.

If the event is something more complicated or larger-scale (tournament, a-thon, or fair), there may be another set of registration tables needed, this one for supervisors, referees, athletes, vendors, and sponsors. It's best to separate their check-in from that of the spectators. They need different things and may be arriving at different times. You may need to give them their own registration forms, gifts, and information packets.

The main job of the registration staff is to sign in those attending and make sure guests have paid and know where to go next. If this is an event with fixed seating, everyone should be given something with the number of his or her seat on it. It's a good idea to give guests a slip of paper big enough not to be easily misplaced but small enough to fit in a jacket pocket of small purse. If you are concerned that there might be party crashers, distribute stickers or pins to your guests to identify them so they may reenter easily.

At some events, the registration staff must collect money. Make sure they are equipped to do this and that they have a secure place to keep the money, calculators or adding machines, and lists of those who have not paid.

Registration should never take more than an hour. If you have enough volunteers, each armed with a guest list, this is possible and necessary; people don't want to wait in line for more than a few minutes. All registration staff should be supplied with a printout of everyone who is attending (listed alphabetically and by table). There should be a troubleshooter to handle last-minute changes that inevitably crop up, no matter how good a job your committee does arranging seating. When this happens, a registration worker should immediately direct the person to the troubleshooter who will make sure the problem is resolved. This way, everyone else isn't delayed in the process.

Assigned seating isn't always necessary or desirable. At an auction or informal affair, let guests seat themselves. Registration for open seating takes much less time.

Although many of your registration team may be experienced, it never hurts to practice before the guests arrive. If you have time, conduct a run-through at the event site. If that's not logistically possible, gather everyone for a practice session at someone's home or your office a few days early. Assign some workers to play the parts of impatient guests, or those with registration problems. Teach the staff how to handle these situations. The one thing the workers must remember to do at all times is smile. Then they should apologize to the guest for the problem and escort them to the troubleshooter table, where someone will work with the guest until the problem is resolved.

Teach workers how to tactfully ask for money from those who have not paid. They should politely ask for a check or credit card (if you are accepting them) and, if they have neither with them, guests should be asked to sign a pledge slip to pay.

As with other aspects of the event, try to anticipate problems that might arise. If you use computers, make sure you have printed back-up lists in case the computers conk out.

If the event is lengthy, try to arrange shifts for registration workers. Don't leave someone on duty for more than an hour or two at a time because registration is a tiring job.

Try to reward registration workers by giving them a good table at the event, giving them the meal free (if you can afford to), or at least making sure they get to see the show without charge.

Consider renting beepers or portable phones for your key staff and registration desk. They make it a lot easier to communicate— with one another as well as the vendor who hasn't shown up on time. If a problem arises, you can easily be reached on a portable phone. These are particularly handy in large outdoor facilities. If your budget can handle it, it's a good investment.

CHECKLIST

☐ The day before the event, check with key committee chairmen and vendors to make sure they know when to arrive.

☐ Pack everything you will need the day before.

☐ If the event is at a hotel, check in a day ahead to set up a temporary control room.

☐ Run through registration procedure with workers before the event.

☐ Set up registration area.

Chapter 10

After Words

Whether your event was a success or a failure, it can provide you with valuable lessons for the future. After everyone has recovered—at least one week but not more than one month after the event—gather the key committee people together to celebrate the event's conclusion, take stock of how things went, and determine what could be improved.

As a token of appreciation for the committee members' hard work, it's nice to have the gathering over lunch at a restaurant or at someone's home. If you didn't thank these people publicly at the event itself (which you should have) this is the place to do it.

When inviting them, let them know there will be a brief run-through of the event. This does not have to be a tense meeting. In fact, take extra care not to blame anyone for anything that went wrong. Stick to what specifically went awry and how it can be prevented from doing so again. Take along a sheet listing the headings and questions—then someone just needs to jot down the answers. Afterwards, have it typed up and distribute it to everyone on the committee. (Don't forget one for the loose-leaf notebook.) This form becomes your working paper for the next event.

TIP: This is also a good time to enlist committee members for the next event.

A sample post-event evaluation questionnaire follows.

POST-EVENT EVALUATION

Event

Was it a good choice?
Did people enjoy themselves?
Did it attract the audience you targeted? If not, why?
What could be changed to improve it?
Did it conflict with another big event?
Should it be held during the day instead of at night, or vice versa?
Was it a fund-raising or friend-raising event?
How many people attended? Was that enough to make it worthwhile? Are more likely to attend the next time?
Did you achieve your fund-raising goal?
Did you attract new donors?
Did you need a rain date?
Did the date set give you enough time to organize and promote the event?
Was the event at the best time of year?

Budget

Did you stay within your guidelines?
How much did the event cost?
Was the amount you spent consistent with your organization's image and goals?
Did the amount you raised warrant such an event?
Did you have enough front money? Adequate cash flow?
Was the bookkeeping done so that all expenses and income were recorded and all money due the organization collected?
Were all bills paid on time?
Were contracts negotiated so as to maximize profit?

Were there items missing from the budget?
If you were to do this again, how could you cut expenses?
Is there anything you might want to add?
Were there any financial surprises?

Event Management

Was your manager able to handle all aspects of the event?
Emergencies? Personalities? Contract negotiations? Delegation of
authority?
Was he/she readily available as problems arose?
Did he/she make assignments clear and follow up on their
progress?
Did he/she need more clerical or bookkeeping help?

Committees

Did they complete assignments?
Were tasks done in a timely manner and within budget?
Did the chairman communicate regularly with the events
manager?
Did they ask for guidance/assistance when needed?
Were there enough/too many people on each committee?
Did the committees meet regularly enough/too often?
Have any new leaders emerged from within the committees?

Location

Was your site the best one for the event?
Did it accommodate the number of people you were expect-
ing?
Might you need a larger or smaller site the next time?
Was weather a consideration?
Was the equipment available there adequate (enough tables,
chairs, kitchen facilities)?

Could this event have been held at a less expensive site or in a less expensive form?

Was the site convenient for those attending?

Was there access to public transportation?

Was there adequate parking at a reasonable price?

Were there many permits required?

Entertainment

Did it enhance the event?

Was it appropriate to the theme?

Was it within the budget?

Did people dance (if there was a band) or like the show?

Were the sound and light systems adequate and functioning properly?

Could better entertainment have been obtained at the same price?

Were contracts properly negotiated?

Did you take full advantage of the publicity potential of well-known entertainers?

Were you able to get housing, transportation, and other entertainment-related costs donated or underwritten?

Could you have done without the underwriting?

Food

How was it?

Were there any complaints about the meal or the service?

How was the presentation?

If your group cooked, did you have enough people and did they all know their jobs?

Did you meet the budget?

Could it have been done less expensively by hiring someone else to do it?

Were you able to accommodate those with special dietary restrictions?

Were there enough beverages/liquor?

Is there any way to save money on food and beverages next time that you didn't use this time?

Publicity

Did you have enough lead time to produce the publicity you wanted?

Did publicity get to the right sources?

How could you have attracted more publicity?

If publicity was handled by a staff person, did he/she need more help?

If done by volunteers, might they have benefited from some professional guidance?

Did you stay within your budget?

Were mailings sent out in a timely manner?

Was there good follow-up?

Were the invitations/fliers/posters attractive?

Were the mailing lists up to date? (If you got a lot returned, you need to update the list.)

Registration

Did it go smoothly?

Was the registration table easy to find?

Was there enough staff to prevent long lines?

Any major problems? Complaints from guests?

Were volunteers appropriately dressed and courteous?

If you used computers, did they function properly?

Chapter 11

Tools of the Trade

Now that you know how to create a great special event, here are some expert sources and resources you can use to make it even better.

PROFESSIONAL ORGANIZATIONS/PUBLISHERS
Fund Raising and General Special Events

American Association of Fund Raising Counsel
25 West 43rd Street
New York, New York 10036
(212) 354-5799
FAX (212) 768-1795
Professional organization of fund-raising professionals. Publishes *Giving USA,* an annual guide that contains national statistics on fund raising and fund-raising trends.

American Council for the Arts
1285 Avenue of the Americas, Third Floor
New York, New York 10019
(212) 245-4510
FAX (212) 245-4514
Publishes an association newsletter and a number of journals. Runs reference library with information on how to hold arts-related events.

American Hospital Publishing Company
211 East Chicago Avenue, Suite 700
Chicago, Illinois 60611
(312) 951-1100
FAX (312) 951-8491
Publishes materials for hospital management professionals, including *The Volunteer Leader,* a monthly publication that focuses on how to administer hospital-related volunteer programs, deal with volunteers, and organize events.

American Management Association
135 West 50th Street
New York, New York 10020
(212) 586-8100
FAX (212) 903-8168
American Management Association's Trainers Workshop, available through this trade group for management professionals, runs a subsidiary that publishes *Trainer's Workshop,* a monthly publication. Each issue focuses on an aspect of management. It comes with lecture materials, group exercises, and handouts you can use to run your own training session. It can be ordered by contacting: Trainers Workshop, P.O. Box 319, Trudeau Road, Saranac Lake, New York 12983. Phone (518) 891-1500. FAX (518) 891-0368.

Association for Health Care Philanthropy
313 Park Avenue, Suite 400
Falls Church, Virginia 22046
(703) 532-6243
FAX (703) 532-7170
A professional group offering education and networking for health care professionals.

Business Committee for the Arts, Inc.
1775 Broadway, Suite 510
New York, New York 10019
(212) 664-0600
FAX (212) 956-5980
Encourages businesses to support the arts. Offers many publications and a quarterly newsletter.

Council for Advancement and Support of Education (CASE)
11 Dupont Circle, Suite 400
Washington, D.C. 20036
(202) 328-5936 or 5996
FAX (202) 387-4973
An organization geared mainly toward colleges and private schools.
It publishes *CASE Currents,* a magazine that offers ideas for special
events. Also publishes various books and runs seminars in various
locales and at various levels, for beginners through seasoned professionals.

Chronicle of Philanthropy
1255 Twenty-third Street, N.W.
Washington, D.C. 20037
(202) 466-1200
FAX (202) 296-2691
A biweekly newspaper for the nonprofit world. It includes news
and information on fund raisers. Almost every issue has a column
about special events. An index of previously published articles is
available.

Community Concerts
165 West 57th Street
New York, New York 10019-2276
(212) 397-6900
FAX (212) 841-9778
A nonprofit organization located in 600 cities in the United States
and Canada. It helps community groups book and promote musical
events, including fund raisers.

Council of Better Business Bureaus
Philanthropic Advisory Service
1515 Wilson Boulevard
Arlington, Virginia 22209
(703) 276-0100
FAX (703) 525-8277
A national clearinghouse of information on nonprofit organizations. Sets standards for nonprofit organizations. Offers many
publications, reports on charities.

Foundation Center, The
79 Fifth Avenue
New York, New York 10003
(212) 620-4230
FAX (212) 691-1828
Offers publications, seminars, a reference library.

Fund Raising Institute
12300 Twinbrook Parkway, Suite 450
Rockville, Maryland 20852
(301) 816-0210
FAX (301) 816-0811
Publishes *FRI Monthly Portfolio,* books on fund raising, philanthropy and nonprofit management, sponsors seminars.

Fundraising Management
Hoke Communications, Inc.
224 Seventh Street
Garden City, New York 11530-5771
(516) 746-6700/(800) 229-6700
Publishes direct marketing and fund raising monthly newsletters. It has an extensive library of printed and video reference materials.

Independent Sector
1828 L Street, N.W.
Washington, D.C. 20036
(202) 223-8100
FAX (202) 467-0609
Nonprofit coalition that encourages charitable giving and voluntarism. Offers many publications.

International Association of Fairs and Expositions
3043 East Cairo
P.O. Box 985
Springfield, Missouri 65801
(417) 862-5771
FAX (417) 862-0156
Provides management of fairs and expositions, offers many catalogs and services. Compiles lists of major fairs and expositions through-

out the United States and in various parts of the world. Fund raisers might use this to find out about events in their area, then seek to tie a fund raiser to them. The group's magazine also includes listings of goods, services, supplies, and entertainment suppliers.

International Events Group
213 West Institute Place, #303
Chicago, Illinois 60610
(312) 944-1727
FAX (312) 944-1897
Compiles *The Official Directory of Festivals, Sports and Special Events* and a biweekly newsletter.

Meeting Planners International
1950 Stemmons Freeway
Dallas, Texas 75207-3109
(214) 746-5224
FAX (214) 746-5248
Professional educational society that serves as a resource for businesses and meeting professionals. Resource center offers information on how to organize meetings and conventions.

Murdock Magazines
500 Plaza Drive, Fifth Floor
Secaucus, New Jersey 07094
(201) 902-1700/(800) 447-7273
FAX (201) 319-1796
Offers a monthly magazine outlining meetings, conventions, and special events.

National Association of Catering Executives
304 West Liberty Street, Suite 201
Louisville, Kentucky 40202
(502) 583-3783
FAX (502) 589-3602
A trade group for food professionals. It operates a certification program for catering executives; a booklet, "Check Before You

Choose," helps laymen shop for a caterer and will refer you to certified association members in cities throughout the country.

National Catholic Development Conference
86 Front Street
Hempstead, New York 11550
(516) 481-6000
FAX (516) 489-9287
A major organization of Catholic groups, publishes many periodicals, including *Fund Raising Forum.*

National Society of Fund Raising Executives (NSFRE)
1101 King Street, Suite 3000
Alexandria, Virginia 22314
(703) 684-0410
FAX (703) 684-0540
Provides guidance and assistance to fund-raising professionals. Publishes a quarterly journal and a newsletter, runs an executive search service.

National Speakers Club
4747 North 7th Street, Suite 310
Phoenix, Arizona 85014
(602) 265-1001
FAX (602) 265-7403
This group is geared toward educating professional speakers.

Non-Profit Times
P.O. Box 408
Hopewell, New Jersey 08525
(609) 466-4600
FAX (609) 466-3388
This monthly publication deals with trends in nonprofit events.

Professional Convention Management Association
100 Vestavia Office Park, Suite 220
Birmingham, Alabama 35216
(205) 823-7262
FAX (205) 822-3891
Publishes bimonthly magazine, *Convene,* which discusses ethics, public speakers, and other topics primarily for convention managers but which could be helpful to nonprofit groups.

Public Relations Society of America
33 Irving Place, Third Floor
New York, New York 10003
(212) 995-2230
FAX (212) 995-0757
Offers a number of periodicals and books and runs a job bank.

Society for Nonprofit Organizations
6314 Odana Road, Suite 1
Madison, Wisconsin 53719
(608) 274-9777
FAX (608) 271-4406
This group offers a variety of books and periodicals to help nonprofit groups.

Special Events Magazine
Miramar Publishing Company
2048 Cotner Avenue
Los Angeles, California 90025
(800) 543-4116/(213) 477-1003
A monthly magazine that also publishes an annual product and source guide.

Taft Group, The
12300 Twinbrook Parkway, Suite 450
Rockville, Maryland 20852
(301) 816-0210
FAX (301) 816-0811
A publishing company offering a variety of books, directories and newsletters for fund raisers and nonprofit groups, including the *Taft Foundation Reporter,* the *Taft Corporate Giving Directory,* and *Who's Wealthy in America.*

Toastmasters International
P.O. Box 10400
2200 N. Grand Avenue
Santa Ana, California 92711
(714) 858-8255
FAX (714) 858-1027
Trains speakers for nonprofit education leadership and communications. Offers many publications.

CELEBRITY SPECIAL EVENTS RESOURCE LIST

Billboard's International Talent & Touring Directory
P.O. Box 2071
Mahopac, New York 10541-2071
(212) 764-7300

Christensen's Ultimate Movie, TV and Rock 'n' Roll
(Annual publication)
Cardiff-by-the-Sea Publishing Company
6065 Mission Gorge Road
San Diego, California 92120
(619) 286-6902

Collector's Book Store
1708 North Vine Street
Hollywood, California 90028
(213) 467-3296

Cavalcade of Acts and Attractions
(Weekly publication)
Amusement Business
Subscription Department
P.O. Box 2072
Mahopac, New York 10541-9954
(212) 536-5133
Guide to performing talent, touring shows, booking agents, personal managers, promoters, and special attractions. International newsweekly: up-to-the-minute news on the mass entertainment and sports industry.

Celebrity Service International, Inc.
(Annual publication)

Patsy Maharam	Jeff Kormos
Celebrity Service International, Inc.	Celebrity Service International, Inc.
1780 Broadway, Suite 300	8833 Sunset Boulevard, Suite 401
New York, New York 10019	
(212) 245-1460	Los Angeles, California 90069
	(213) 652-9910

A data bank of more than 300,000 names of celebrities and newsmakers.

Five major services provided only to subscribers:
- Daily Bulletin—a daily tracking of the whereabouts of celebrities, including how to contact them.
- Telephone Service—a daily phone service to gain instant information on major personalities.
- International Social Calendar—a listing of international social events for partygoers, charities, social planners, and jet setters.
- Theatrical Calendar—an informative compilation of theatrical activities, including openings, productions, and casting opportunities.
- Special Services—a division that handles activities relating to openings and new products, including the appearance of celebrities at business, charity, and fund-raising events.

Two indispensable publications:
- *Celebrity Register*—the encyclopedia of newsmakers and stars. More than 1,600 celebrity biographies with individual photographs.
- *Contact Book*—a concise, comprehensive directory of the top personalities and organizations dealing with the entertainment industry for eight major cities: New York, San Francisco, Hollywood, Washington, Toronto, London, Paris, and Rome.

Variety
(Weekly publication)
475 Park Avenue South
New York, New York 10016
(212) 779-1100
The standard trade magazine for the entertainment field.

Hollywood Studio Blue Book
6715 Sunset Boulevard
Hollywood, California 90028
(213) 464-7411
Comprehensive listing for anything in Hollywood, including production, advertising, filmmakers, personal managers, and celebrities.

CELEBRITY SOURCES

American Federation of Television and Radio Artists (AFTRA)
6922 Hollywood Boulevard, 8th Floor
Hollywood, California 90028
(213) 461-8111
or
1350 Avenue of the Americas
New York, New York 10019
(212) 265-7700

American Society of Composers, Authors and Publishers
    (ASCAP)
1 Lincoln Plaza
New York, New York 10023
(212) 595-3050

Broadcast Music Inc. (BMI)
320 West 57th Street
New York, New York 10019
(212) 586-2000

The Conference of Personal Managers, Inc.
201 North Robertson Boulevard, Suite A
Beverly Hills, California 90211-1799
(213) 275-2456

Screen Actors Guild (SAG)
7065 Hollywood Boulevard
Los Angeles, California 90028
(213) 465-4600
or
1700 Broadway
New York, New York 10019
(212) 957-5370

FULL SERVICE PRODUCTION COMPANIES
Very Big Budget Super Extravaganzas

Radio City Music Hall Productions
1210 Avenue of the Americas   2049 Century Park East
Rockefeller Center, Suite 1200   Los Angeles, California 90067
New York, New York 10020   (213) 551-2721
(212) 246-4600
Large-scale international and national events, comprehensive planning and implementation. Creates one-time events as well as those with ongoing potential.

Walt Disney World Creative Entertainment
P.O. Box 10,000
Lake Buena Vista, Florida 32830
(407) 345-5772
Handles very large-scale events.

MODERATE TO LARGE EVENTS, CONCERTS, AND FUND RAISERS

Ray Block Productions
Attention: Ed Yoe
666–11th Street, N.W., Suite 1002
Washington, D.C. 20001
(202) 347-SHOW
FAX (202) 638-3055
This company produces all sorts of special events, including banquets, charity balls, concerts, fashion shows, theme parties, celebrity auctions, golf tournaments, lectures, and symposia.

SPEAKER BUREAUS

Harry Walker Inc.
3616 Empire State Building
350 Fifth Avenue
New York, New York 10118
(212) 563-0700
The nation's foremost people, including former presidents, economists, media (Ted Koppel, Tom Brokaw, John Chancellor), news-

paper columnists (Ann Landers), political figures, and other individuals from the worlds of show business, religion, and sports, can be booked through this firm.

The Nelson Agency
170 East 79th Street
New York, New York 10021
(212) 744-0262
Exclusive agency for celebrated speakers in the arts and letters.

BOOK REFERENCES

Alberti, Charles E., George S. Macko, and Nike B. Whitcomb. *Money Makers: A Systematic Approach to Special Events Fund Raising* (Madison, Wisconsin: Society for Nonprofit Organizations).

Beatty, Betsy, and Libby Kirkpatrick. *The Auction Book* (Denver: Auction Press, 1983).

Brentlinger, Marilyn E., and Judith M. Weiss. *The Ultimate Benefit Book: How to Raise $50,000 Plus for Your Organization* (Cleveland: Octavia Press, 1987).

Brody, Ralph, and Marcia Goodman. *Fund-Raising Events: Strategies and Programs for Success* (Cleveland: Human Sciences Press, 1988).

Devney, Darcy Champion. *Organizing Special Events and Conferences: A Practical Guide for Busy Volunteers and Staff* (Sarasota, Florida: Pineapple Press, 1990).

Drotning, Phillip T. *500 Ways for Small Charities to Raise Money* (Washington: Public Service Materials Center, 1981).

Dunn, Thomas G. *How to Shake the Money Tree: Creative Fund-Raising for Today's Nonprofit Organizations* (New York: Viking Penguin, 1988).

Geir, Ted. *Make Your Events Special* (New York: Folkwork the Public Interest Production Company, 1986).

Harris, April L. *Special Events: Planning for Success* (Washington: Council for Advancement and Support of Education, 1988).

Kraatz, Katie, and Julie Haynes. *The Fundraising Formula: 50*

Creative Events Proven Successful Nationwide (Rockville, Maryland: Fund Raising Institute, 1987).

Lagauskas, Valerie. *Parades: How to Plan, Promote and Stage Them* (New York: Sterling Publishing Co., Inc., 1982).

Lawrence, Elizabeth. *The Complete Caterer: A Practical Guide to the Craft and Business of Being a Caterer* (New York: Doubleday, 1988).

Miller, Donna. *A Guide to Catering: Catering Your Own Events or Hiring Professionals* (Portland, Oregon: DJ's Guides, 1986).

Ninkovich, Thomas. *Reunion Handbook: A Guide for School & Military Reunions,* 2nd Edition Reunion Research (San Francisco: 1989).

Plessner, Gerald M. *The Encyclopedia of Fundraising: Golf Tournament Management Manual* Fund Raisers Inc. (Arcadia, California: 1986).

Plessner, Gerald M. *The Encyclopedia of Fundraising: Charity Auction Management Manual* Fund Raisers Inc. (Arcadia, California: 1986).

Plessner, Gerald. *The Encyclopedia of Fundraising: Testimonial Dinner and Industry Luncheon Management Manual,* Fund Raisers Inc. (Arcadia, California, 1980).

Setterberg, Fred, and Kary Schulman. *Beyond Profit: The Complete Guide to Managing the Nonprofit Organization* (New York: Harper & Row Publishers Inc., 1985).

Sheerin, Mira. *How to Raise Top Dollars from Special Events* (Hartsdale, New York: Public Service Materials Center, 1984).

Acknowledgments

Writing this book was a lot like producing a special event: It took a while to develop the idea and a lot of research and consultation before I decided to do it. I got the idea in 1980, when through my work with the National Parkinson Foundation, I met Richard B. Stolley, then managing editor of *Life* magazine. He saw what I did and, over the course of several years, repeatedly asked me why I hadn't written a book about it.

Finally, during the summer of 1989, I found myself in the enviable position of having some spare time. Dick Stolley again reminded me that this was a prime opportunity to write a book. While I knew enough about special events to do this, I wasn't so sure I could write about it. But my experience in special events taught me to rely on experts.

My sister, Susan Freedman, and I often discuss our problems and projects. I asked if she knew anyone who could help me make it worthwhile and readable. She introduced me to Karen Feldman Smith. Karen, a newspaper writer and editor, turned out to be the ideal writing partner. During the two years we worked together, despite the often long hours and sometimes difficult work, the experience was mainly one of joy and learning. This book could not have happened without Karen's help, suggestions, prodding, questions and all the good things a reporter does.

This book probably wouldn't have happened without the patience and computer expertise of Karen's husband, Gregg, who put up with my ever more frequent stays at their home and daily phone calls.

Special thanks are due to several friends, all experts in the fields of special events and entertainment, who read the initial drafts and gave freely of their knowledge and opinions: Bonnie Nelson Schwartz, Blossom K. Horowitz, Milton B. Suchin and Hank Lione.

Special thanks also to Chuck Lean and Jean Bernard at FRI, and to Celia Chin Quee for typing the initial manuscript.

The celebrities who have taught me my craft are too numerous to mention, but I'm especially grateful to: Bob and Dolores Hope, Dick and Kari Clark, Phyllis Diller, Aretha Franklin, Bill Harris, Elizabeth Taylor, Patti LaBelle, Peter Max, Estelle Getty, Cab Calloway, Marvin Hamlisch, Delta Burke and Ann Jillian.

A project like this would never happen without the encouragement and support of colleagues and friends including: David Sullivan, Roni and Gary Harkey, Sylvia Bennett Sawelson, Sherry and Ron Funt, Celia Lipton Farris, Dwight Meyer, Sue Weiss, Peter Alper and Ed Yoe. I owe a special thank you to my friend Dr. Nina Pearlmutter, who was always there for me.

And, of course, I owe thanks to my parents, Benjamin Feir and Dr. Irene Schaeffer Feir, who always encouraged me in everything I do. Special love and thanks to my son, Brian Freedman, who makes every day a truly special event.

—Harry Freedman

My thanks to:

—my long-time friend, Susan Freedman, who knows a good match when she sees it.

—my friend and collaborator, Harry Freedman, whose knowledge, efficiency and patience made this as angst-free a project as I've ever worked on.

—my long-suffering husband, Gregg, who encouraged me to tackle this project and was unwaveringly supportive througnout it.

—my parents, Jerry and Adele Feldman, who gave me the confidence and skills I needed to become a writer.

—my friends, Ad Hudler and Ed Clement, who told me this project would be good for me. They were right.

—Karen Feldman Smith

Index

About the Authors

Harry A. Freedman is a member of the development staff of the University of Miami School of Medicine and executive director of The Transplant Foundation of South Florida. He is nationally recognized for producing large-scale special events, often featuring big-name celebrities. These events have generated more than $25 million during the past ten years. In 1987, he was recognized by *Forbes* magazine for his innovative fund-raising efforts.

Freedman is a member of the National Society of Fund Raising Executives and speaks frequently on topics such as special events marketing for charities, major donor fund raising, and the cultivation of volunteers. Freedman has been a fund raiser for the past ten years, following a career as an educational psychologist helping children with learning disabilities. He is a single parent and resides in Miami, Florida.

Karen Feldman Smith is a journalist based in Fort Myers, Florida. Her works have appeared in newspapers throughout the United States and Canada. She is a graduate of Franklin and Marshall College and the Graduate School of Journalism of Columbia University.